ESSENTIAL MESSAGES FROM GOD'S SERVANTS

master*Work*®

Lessons from

GOD, DO YOU REALLY CARE?

by Tony Evans

HE SPEAKS TO ME

by Priscilla Shirer

SUMMER *2008*

LifeWay.
Biblical Solutions for Life

Ross H. McLaren, *Editor in Chief*

Wanda King, *Editor*

Carolyn B. Gregory, *Copy Editor*

David Wilson, *Graphic Designer*

Melissa Finn, *Lead Technical Specialist*

Alan Raughton
Lead Adult Ministry Specialist

David Apple
Adult Ministry Specialist

Send questions/comments to
  Editor, *MasterWork*
  One LifeWay Plaza
  Nashville, TN 37234-0175
  Or make comments on the web at
  www.lifeway.com

Management Personnel

Bret Robbe, *Director*
Leadership and Adult Publishing
Ron Brown, Larry Dry, Ron Keck
Managing Directors
Leadership and Adult Publishing
David Francis, *Director*
Sunday School
Bill Craig, *Director*
Leadership and Adult Ministry
Gary Hauk, *Director Publishing*
LifeWay Church Resources

Lessons by Tony Evans are condensed from *God, Do You Really Care?* (Sisters, Ore: Multnomah Publishers, 2006). Used by permission of Random House Publishers. All rights reserved.

Lessons by Priscilla Shirer are condensed from *He Speaks to Me* (Nashville: LifeWay Press, 2005). © LifeWay Press. Used by permission. All rights reserved.

MasterWork: Essential Messages from God's Servants (ISSN 1542-703X, Item 005075042) is published quarterly by LifeWay Christian Resources of the Southern Baptist Convention, One LifeWay Plaza, Nashville, Tennessee 37234; Thom S. Rainer, President. © Copyright 2008 LifeWay Christian Resources of the Southern Baptist Convention.

For ordering or inquiries, visit *www.lifeway.com*, or write LifeWay Church Resources Customer Service, One LifeWay Plaza, Nashville, TN 37234-0113. For subscriptions or subscription address changes, e-mail *subscribe@lifeway.com*, fax (615) 251-5818, or write to the above address. For bulk shipments mailed quarterly to one address, e-mail *orderentry@lifeway.com*, fax (615) 251-5933, or write to the above address.

Printed in the United States of America.

Cover photo credit:
© Comstock Images/Jupiterimages Unlimited

table of Contents

God, Do You Really Care?

As a minister of the gospel of Jesus Christ, I'm often asked whether God really cares. Does He care when people are sick, injured, and dying? Does He care when they grieve over death—the death of loved ones, the death of their own goals and dreams? Does God concern Himself when people, even people who didn't have much to begin with, lose everything? Is He moved when men and women are confused and lost, picking through the rubble and devastation of their lives?

Why would God allow such suffering? Could He really be the loving Heavenly Father He's been made out to be? Doesn't He seem more like a passive bystander to our pain sometimes? Truth be told, it can sometimes look—within human reasoning anyway—as though God doesn't really care all that much that people are suffering.

In the midst of such events, we all need the answer to one key question: Does God care when we hurt? I've written these lessons to answer you unequivocally: *Yes, He cares!*

Tony Evans

ABOUT THE WRITERS

Tony Evans

is the senior pastor of Oak Cliff Bible Fellowship and president of The Urban Alternative, a national ministry that equips the church to promote clear understanding and relevant application of Scripture to urban communities. He is the author of numerous books, including *The Promise, What Matters Most, Returning to Your First Love, The Battle Is the Lord's,* and *Free at Last.*

JOE BECKLER wrote the personal learning activities and teaching plans for this study. Joe holds a Master of Divinity degree from New Orleans Baptist Theological Seminary. Currently he is planting a church in Durango, Colorado. He enjoys participating in outdoor sports. Joe and his wife Cheri also parent triplet sons.

ABOUT THIS STUDY

Typically, what is your first reaction when you are experiencing any level of suffering? Place the number 1 next to that response. Then number your second and third responses in numerical order.

___ I feel abandoned by God.
___ I wonder if God really cares.
___ I cry out to God for help.
___ I stoically embrace suffering as a part of life.
___ Other: _____

master*Work*:
Essential Messages from God's Servants

• Designed for developing and maturing believers who desire to go deeper into the spiritual truths of God's Word.

• Ideal for many types of Bible study groups.

• A continuing series from leading Christian authors and their key messages.

• Based on LifeWay's well-known, interactive model for daily Bible study.

• The interspersed interactive personal learning activities **in bold type** are written by the writer identified on the Study Theme unit page.

• Teaching plans follow each lesson to help facilitators guide learners through lessons.

• Published quarterly.

"Arouse Yourself, why do You sleep, O Lord? Awake, do not reject us forever. Why do You hide Your face and forget our affliction and our oppression? For our soul has sunk down into the dust; Our body cleaves to the earth" (Ps. 44:23–25).

God, Do You Really Care ... When I'm Sick?

day One

Jesus Loves Me, Yet . . .

Over the course of my ministry, I've spent time with hundreds of believers whose bodies have been afflicted by illness and injury. In the wake of those physical setbacks and seasons of pain, I often hear questions like these:

- *If God really loves me, why is He allowing me to suffer this way?*
- *Is God paying attention? What is He going to do for me now that I'm sick?*
- *Where is God when I'm sick and need Him most?*
- *Why doesn't God just step in and heal me?*

Which of the above questions reflects how you feel when calamity has struck your life or the life of someone close to you?

When we or a loved one is sick, it's easy to question whether God cares because, frankly, it's at those times when it seems He doesn't. In our human thinking, if He was truly concerned about us, He wouldn't allow us to go on suffering that way.

The Bible is filled with declarations of God's loving, caring heart for those who suffer. But I want to focus our attention on an account in which Jesus demonstrates over and over just how much He cares for those He loves. It's the account of the sickness and physical death of a man named

Lazarus—and the stunning miracle Jesus performed on his behalf and on the behalf of his sisters, Mary and Martha.

After reading John11:1-3, list three things that caught your attention in the passage.

1. _____

2. _____

3. _____

John, you'll notice, goes out of his way to tell us that Jesus loved Lazarus. This wasn't just brotherly love for a fellow human being but a personal, heartfelt love. Jesus loved Lazarus with the love of God, the one and only perfect love—what the Bible calls *agape* love.

Yet Lazarus wasn't just sick; he was gravely ill. In the original language of John's Gospel, the word *sick* refers to a sickness leading to death. In other words, Lazarus was dying.

Do you think it's easy to know when "God allows" something, such as illness, to happen for a greater purpose? Explain your response.

_____

_____

This demonstrates something we all need to keep in mind: It is possible for Jesus to love us and for us to love Him in return and still get sick—even deathly sick. Not only that, but there are times when God allows us to become sick for specific purposes in His great (and often incomprehensible) plan.

In the case of Lazarus, someone Jesus loved had fallen deathly ill. And it was a situation that was going to get a lot worse before it got better.

day Two

From Bad to Worse

Faced with a problem beyond their ability to fix, Mary and Martha sent word to Jesus. This is a simple but beautiful example of what prayer really is—taking our problems or situations to the Father through Jesus Christ, and humbly asking Him to provide the remedy we could never provide.

Obviously Mary and Martha wanted Jesus to come to Bethany right away and heal their brother. To them, it was a simple formula of Jesus' love and their request equaling healing for Lazarus.

But it didn't happen that way.

Jesus did not drop everything He was doing and go to Lazarus immediately. He stayed two more days where He was—in Perea. The Gospels call Perea "the land beyond the Jordan." It was about 40 miles from Bethany, which was about two miles east of Jerusalem. Instead, of coming immediately, Jesus sent these words of assurance: "This sickness is not to end in death, but for the glory of God, that the Son of God may be glorified by it" (John 11:4).

Strictly from an earthly perspective, would you feel reassured by Jesus' response in John 11:4? Why or why not? _____

Meanwhile, Lazarus didn't get well. In fact, his condition only worsened. And Jesus wouldn't show up in Bethany until it was—in Mary and Martha's minds anyway—too late. By the time He would arrive, Lazarus would have been dead and buried.

In our human thinking, that doesn't sound very much like a Savior who cared when His close friend became sick, does it? Jesus had already proven over and over that He had the supernatural ability to do something about Lazarus's sickness.

So … He had the ability. He loved Lazarus. He loved Mary and Martha. The sisters had exercised simple faith in asking Him to come. But He did nothing, and their beloved brother was slipping away.

When we are faced with sickness, we tend to believe—probably as Mary and Martha did—that if God truly cared He would step in and do something about it. But it doesn't always happen that way. In fact, our situation may stay the same—or even become worse.

Certainly God has the ability to heal us in an instant, but just as certainly there are many times when He doesn't. *But that doesn't mean He doesn't care,* and Jesus' words for Mary and Martha's messengers demonstrate that fact.

Revisit Jesus' words in John 11:4. Based on a God-empowered perspective, how do Jesus' words exhibit a sense of hope? _____

A Personal Word

Jesus didn't give Mary and Martha the immediate solution they had asked in faith to receive. But He didn't remain silent about it either. He didn't leave His friends "twisting in the wind."

Jesus demonstrated how much He cared about Mary and Martha—as well as their sick brother—when He gave them something God wants to give each of us today—a personal word.

When Jesus told these ladies, "This sickness is not unto death, but for the glory of God, that the Son of God may be glorified by it," He wasn't talking about sickness in general. Jesus started out His promise to Mary and Martha with the phrase "*This* sickness," meaning that He was speaking specifically to *them* and to *their* situation.

The same is true for us today.

Based on your experience, has God felt personal or impersonal to you? Mark your response on the continuum below.

Impersonal   **Personal**

What has contributed to feeling this way?

_____

When you are sick and hurting, it's vitally important to hear what God has to say to you in the midst of your situation. In other words, you need to hear a personal word from God. While many Christians today hear the Word *of* God, I wonder how many really hear a word *from* God. By that I mean that while they may know the Bible well and are fully aware of God's promises, they have never personalized it, never taken the time to read and study it, and then ask God, "What are you saying *to me personally* through Your Word?"

Describe a time when God gave you a personal message through His word. _____

What did He reveal to you? _____

In the margin, write down what was happening in your life at the time you received this personal word.

Caring for Us Through Others

Even though Lazarus was sick to the point of physical death, he wasn't alone in his illness. On the contrary, he faced his sickness within the context of a caring earthly family and a caring spiritual family—an earthly family because his sisters were with him and a spiritual family because they loved Jesus.

Lazarus didn't need to send for his friend and Lord in his illness; Mary and Martha took care of that. And the message they sent to Jesus in Perea was based on two things: their love for their brother ... and their belief that Jesus loved them and could do something about their sick brother.

How do we know these things about Mary and Martha?

The answer is found in John 11:2, which tells us something about Mary that at first might escape our attention. She is specifically described as the one who "anointed the Lord with ointment, and wiped His feet with her hair."

John wrote his Gospel several decades after Jesus' death and resurrection, and when he tells us that Mary was the one who had anointed Jesus with oil, he was referring to an incident recorded one chapter later, just days before Jesus would finally enter into Jerusalem for the final time.

In the culture of that time and place, anointing someone's feet was an outward expression of adoration, even worship. When Mary anointed Jesus' feet, she was expressing her love and adoration, an act Jesus not only allowed but encouraged (see John 12:7–8). This shows us something about Mary's relationship with Jesus: She had a special connection with Him, and she didn't care what others thought as she openly worshiped Him.

When we are sick or hurting and can't make a "prayer connection" with God, He uses others to demonstrate how much He cares for us. It is during those times that we need to be close to somebody who knows how to get close to Jesus, someone who regularly sits at His feet and worships Him.

That's what the apostle James was referring to when he wrote the instructions in James 5:14-15. Look up these verses and indicate what James told his readers to do if they were sick.

_____

What would the results of such action be? _____

_____

Why should we call the elders to pray for us? Because when we are sick, it may be difficult if not impossible for us to pray for ourselves. Beyond that fact, if sin is the root cause of our sickness, we may be blinded from even seeing it. In that case, it is good for us to be able to call on those who, like Mary, are in close fellowship with God, those who sit at His feet and know what to ask Him for.

Who do you call on to support and care for you in hard times? _____

Why this person (or group of people)? _____

When we are in sick or in need, God wants to give us a personal word. But as we study God's *written* Word and seek His *personal* word to us in our situations, we need to understand that He may not tell us everything we want to know in advance.

When God Doesn't Tell Us Everything

> "The fact is, while Mary and Martha had a personal word from Jesus, they did not have access to all the plans in His heart. No human being has that."
> —Tony Evans

The Lord's personal word to Mary and Martha was a message of great comfort and assurance. After all, this was Jesus talking. Mary and Martha both knew Him well and knew all about His teaching and His miracles. If anyone's words concerning their brother could be trusted, they were His.

But if we look at the timing of Jesus receiving word of Lazarus's illness, combined with the timing of His departure from Perea to Bethany (a good two-days' journey), it appears almost certain that Lazarus was already dead by the time the two sisters received His word. Not only that, but it's entirely possible that Lazarus was dead by the time Jesus received word of the illness.

I can't help but wonder at the confusion Mary and Martha felt when they received Jesus' personal word that "this sickness is not unto death." Those words must have rung just a little bit hollow! I can just imagine them hearing that message, then looking at their brother's dead body and wondering if Jesus knew what He was talking about … or if He really cared about their predicament.

In the margin describe a time when you felt like "hope" arrived too late.

The fact is, while Mary and Martha had a personal word from Jesus, they did not have access to all the plans in His heart. No human being has that. The sisters couldn't know the particulars of how Jesus was going to work in their brother's situation. He didn't tell them.

That's how hearing a personal word from God sometimes works, even today. As we pray for a word from God or for an outright healing or deliverance, we need to understand that there will be times when God's response leaves lots of blanks on the page. The understanding He gives us may be "part 1" of 10 parts … or of 100 parts. In other words, He may want us to receive enlightenment in a step-by-step or progressive way.

In the margin describe a time when you felt like God's enlightenment came in a "step-by-step" way.

First of all, God in His infinite wisdom knows that we wouldn't be able to handle knowing everything He had planned for us all at once. We might find ourselves tempted to move out ahead of Him—to accomplish by ourselves what He has planned to do for us.

Second, if He revealed everything to us up front, that would keep us from learning to trust Him and to have absolute faith that He is in control.

I believe that is partly why Jesus didn't fill in the blanks when it came to what He planned to do about Lazarus's sickness. Had He told Mary and Martha from the beginning that Lazarus would die, be buried, and then be raised from the dead, it's likely they wouldn't have learned the lessons about faith that Jesus wanted these two, dear, grieving women to learn.

When God gives us a personal word in our suffering, we don't *need* all the details up front. It's enough to know that the great Creator of the universe cares enough to speak to us *individually*.

But Why Just a Word?

Jesus had sent Mary and Martha a personal word, and it was a personal word designed to expand and strengthen their faith and trust in Him. But that leaves us with some important questions: Why didn't Jesus just go to Bethany immediately and do for Mary and Martha what they had requested—and expected?

When Jesus finally arrived in Bethany, a bitterly disappointed and grieving Martha greeted Him at the outskirts of town and cried, "Lord, if You had been here, my brother would not have died" (John 11:21). In Martha's mind—and in the mind of her sister, who a short time later said the very same thing—it was too late for Jesus to do anything about her brother's sickness.

But within the realm of the Heavenly Father's perfect plan, Jesus arrived right on time. You see, there was more to be done than a simple healing or resurrection. Jesus wanted to teach some people He loved very dearly what it meant to trust and obey Him, even in the worst of situations. For Him to have come to Bethany before He did would have thwarted that plan.

What does it mean for you to "trust and obey" God in the "worst of situations"? _____

How do you believe this is of benefit to you and others? _____

When we or one of our loved ones is sick and hurting, we want God to move, and we want Him to move *right now*. It's quite natural to pray that way, and I don't think it's a bad thing to do so. But it's important that when we pray for God to move for us that we also pray like Job, who endured more than his share of suffering and who said, "Though He slay me, I will hope in Him" (Job 13:15).

Jesus had told the anxious sisters that their brother's sickness would not end in death. While He didn't fill them in on the specifics of His plan and didn't arrive right away like they wanted Him to, He let them know that He was in control and knew how the situation was going to end.

When we or a loved one is going through tough times of illness or other difficulties, we need to keep our eyes on two things: The Lord knows what we're going through, and He knows how our situations will end ... for our good and for His glory.

Think about a situation you or someone you love is facing. What do you want God to be aware of concerning this situation? _____

How could this situation yield results that glorify God?

_____

Before the Session

On a poster board, write out the Introduction interactive (p. 5). If possible, place this poster in a prominent location in front of the class or small group.

During the Session

1. Start the class time by referring to the introduction interactive (p. 5 or written on the poster board). Allow learners to share reactions to this interactive. Explain that the *God, Do You Really Care?* study is designed to encourage us in exploring God's role in the tough situations we face in life.

2. Ask learners to share how they responded to the first interactive of Day 1. Read John 11:1-3. Allow learners to share their responses to the second interactive of Day 1. Explain that it is very important for us to understand the mysterious reality that God sometimes allows hard things to happen and that this is no indication of a lack of love for us. Ask learners to share their responses to the last interactive of Day 1.

3. Read John 11:4 aloud. After reading this verse, ask learners to share how Dr. Evans "unpacked" the verse in Day 2's material. Explain that Jesus wanted Mary and Martha to have a new sense of hope. Ask: *How does John 11:4 offer a sense of hope? Is this the kind of hopeful message you would want to hear?*

4. Ask learners to share how they reacted to the first interactive of Day 3. Ask: *What, if anything, seems personal about Jesus' words in John 11:4? What helps make God personal to you?* Direct learners to look at the last interactive on Day 3. Allow time for learners to share their responses.

5. Explain that the hardest part of suffering often is the isolation we feel as we go through our hurt. Ask: *Who stood with Lazarus as he walked through hard times? Who has stood with you when you've walked through hard times? What type of support did that person (those persons) offer?* Emphasize that Mary and Martha offered Lazarus physical support and spiritual support when he was helplessly sick. Call on a volunteer to read aloud James 5:14-15. Ask learners to share how they responded

Tony Evans's *God, Do You Really Care?* is an extremely applicable study for adults. We all have faced a situation where we felt helpless and wanted God to rescue us. Whether illness, a wayward child, an unpredictable job market, or any assortment of other issues, people wonder where God is when things fall apart in life. The "elephant in the room" is often people's sense of doubt concerning why God doesn't seem to help or intervene in their situation. In this first lesson, help learners identify with their own crisis situations and dilemmas that have prompted them to cry out to God for help.

to the interactives located after the reference to James 5:14-15 on pages 11-12. Explain that God allows us to stand together when someone is hurting. The power of our faith is often found when the church community rallies around us. Ask learners to consider how they could be a "Mary and Martha" to people in and around their lives.

6. As a class, read together the quotation from Tony Evans found in the margin of page 12. Ask: *How much of God's plans do you think we have access to?* Refer to Mary and Martha. Ask learners to consider how these two ladies must have felt as they struggled with Jesus' timing. Allow learners to share their response to the first interactive of Day 5.

7. Ask learners to share their responses to the second interactive in Day 5 on page 13. Reread John 11:4 aloud. Ask: *What does this verse have to say about Jesus' timing?* Refer to the third interactive of Day 5 on page 14. Ask learners to share their understanding of what it means to "trust and obey." Bring the class to a conclusion by discussing the final activity of Day 5 on the bottom of page 14. Allow time for learners to share and to pray concerning some of the situations they listed.

8. In preparation for next week's lesson, ask learners to bring something to class that represents a time when they put themselves in a careless situation. For example, a learner could bring a photo of a river-rafting trip. [These items will be used in the During the Session portion of the lesson.]

God, Do You Really Care ... When I'm Afraid?

day One

We're Going *Where?*

There are some things plain old common sense keeps us from doing because we know better than to intentionally or carelessly put ourselves in harm's way.

In the margin describe a time when you felt you put yourself in a careless situation. Why did you do it?

That's exactly how the twelve disciples saw what Jesus was asking them to do when He said, "Let us go to Judea again" (John 11:7).

Judea was the Roman region of Palestine (now Israel) that included the holy city of Jerusalem as well as the little village of Bethany, where Jesus' close friends Lazarus, Mary, and Martha lived. It was also the hub of Jewish religious life in those days. And at that particular time it was a hotbed of hostility toward Jesus from the religious leadership—those who wanted more than anything to put an end to Him and the "movement" He appeared to be starting.

John records three previous scenes of potential violence against Jesus in Judea.

According to John 5:18, why was the Jewish leadership upset with Jesus? _____

In John 5 the apostle tells us that the Jewish leadership wanted to kill Jesus because He was (at least in their eyes) breaking the Sabbath. But that was only half of it. He had also called God His Father, which in the Jewish faith essentially meant claiming equality with God.

How do people in your life react to the claims of Jesus? _____

In chapter 8 John tells us that the Jews had actually picked up stones to kill Him because He had made this stunning claim: "Truly, truly I say to you, before Abraham was born, I am" (John 8:58). The Jews immediately recognized "I Am" as the name God had used from ancient days to identify Himself as the one and only eternal God. To their ears that sounded like blasphemy, and deserving of death.

Later Jesus was again threatened with stoning during the Feast of Dedication in Jerusalem. And once again it was because of claims He made that the Jews considered blasphemous. A group of Jews had asked Jesus to plainly tell them whether or not He was the Messiah. After pointing out that He already had told them who He really was, Jesus shocked them by saying, "I and the Father are one" (John 10:30).

Now with the desire to kill Him still burning white hot, Jesus told His men that they were going to jump right back into the frying pan. The disciples, however, were in no mood to even think about heading back to Judea, a place they knew wasn't safe. They asked Him, "Rabbi, the Jews were just now seeking to stone You, and are You going there again?" (John 11:8).

Write in the margin what Jesus' willingness to walk into harms way to reach Lazarus revealed about His nature.

day Two

What's All This "Us" Talk?

At a glance the disciples seemed concerned about Jesus' safety. But what they were really doing was camouflaging their own fear under concern for Jesus. When they asked Him, "Are You going back there again?" what they *really* meant was, "Are You taking us back there again?"

The disciples were afraid to go back to Judea. There were people there—people in positions of power and authority—who wanted Jesus dead.

And if they wanted Jesus dead, His closest followers had to believe they wanted *them* dead too.

Where in your life are people most hostile to your faith? _____

Jesus, however, showed no fear at all. He knew He had a great God-ordained appointment to glorify the Father and Himself and to make an impact for the kingdom, and He was intent on obeying God's call.

Jesus' obvious courage in the face of such a clear and deadly threat was a nonverbal lesson for the disciples about the importance of focus. You see, Jesus wasn't focused on the indisputable fact that the Jewish leadership in Judea wanted to kill Him. In fact, He had a focus that overshadowed everything else: He was committed to continuing His life of perfect obedience to the Father no matter what kind of worldly danger it presented. That's because He was completely and perfectly "in tune" with the Father and knew that nothing in the universe could harm Him until the appointed time.

The frightened group of men had a very simple and direct question for Jesus: "Are you really going to Judea?" It was a logical, reasonable question. But Jesus' answer no doubt had them scratching their heads—and probably feeling a bit frustrated: "Are there not twelve hours of daylight? A man who walks by day will not stumble, for he sees by this world's light. It is when he walks by night that he stumbles, for he has no light" (John 11:9–10, NIV).

Now if I had been one of the disciples, I might have asked Jesus what all that talk of light and darkness had to do with the price of camels in Egypt. After all, what I really wanted to know was, "Are You really intending to take us back to a place where we know there are people gunning for You—and probably us too? Can't You answer with a simple yes or no? And while You're at it, why don't You tell us why in the world we would want to go back there, anyway?"

How often do you think we miss out on God's amazing plans simply because we "chicken out"? _____

What typically causes you to cower instead of moving forward with what God asks you to do? _____

When you stuck to it and endured hardship for the sake of following God's will, what happened?

_____

day Three

A Deeper Lesson

Quite often during His earthly ministry Jesus answered very direct questions with what appeared to be elusive or evasive answers. Sometimes it seemed like His answers had nothing at all to do with what was asked. But when He did that, He invariably had a deeper spiritual lesson in His answer than what His questioners might have had in mind. He would sometimes be answering the bigger, nonverbal questions *behind* the question.

Instead of talking to them about the merits of strolling back into the killing zone, He began to speak about what time of day they would be traveling—when there was daylight.

Why do you think Jesus was so concerned with teaching about daylight verses darkness?

_____

At this time in history the Romans had constructed an amazing system of highways and roads throughout the empire, which made travel much easier. But what they couldn't do in that day and age was light those roads for nighttime travel. Because of that, nighttime travel was possible only when there was sufficient moonlight to light the traveler's way.

Obviously, however, Jesus had something more profound in mind than Roman Empire travel tips. He spoke figuratively, using the illuminating light of the sun as an analogy to teach them to put fear in its place.

In the Bible, words such as *day* and *light* refer to God's righteousness—that which is of the Word of God and in the will of God. On the other hand, the words *night* and *darkness* point us toward evil and unrighteousness.

On a daily basis, how many things do you typically encountered as "light"? How about "darkness"? Fill in the chart below with your examples.

LIGHT	DARKNESS

Jesus was seeking to teach His men the spiritual principle of walking in and being governed by the illumination of the light of God. When they did that, He was saying, they didn't need to allow their fears to paralyze them or keep them from courageous obedience.

List in the margin specific fears that have paralyzed you in the past.

How about right now? _____

The bottom line? Jesus Himself was the "daylight" in which His followers must walk. If they were walking with Him, walking in His will, walking in His illumination, walking in His protection, they had nothing to fear from dark or threatening circumstances.

How has walking in the light of Jesus affected your level of confidence? _____

When Jesus recognized that the disciples were frightened at the prospect of heading into Judea, He didn't tell them they would wait until things cooled down and then head out. That would have thwarted the divine appointment He had with Lazarus and his sisters. He didn't allow them to give in to their fears and take a safer course. Instead, He told them they would walk toward Judea and that they would do it during the time when the sun illuminated the road. On such a path, flooded with the light of His presence, they would gain the right perspective on the things that caused them to fear.

Think again about the fears that presently seem to paralyze you. With the illumination of Christ, describe in the margin one way you can move toward overcoming your fears.

Choosing to Walk in the Light

All of us will face things in life that frighten us, but we are only defeated by our fears when we allow them to keep us from staying on the course God has given us to run. God wants us to live a life of fulfillment and joy in Him, but if there is one thing that will keep us from doing that, it's *fear*. Fear holds us back, cripples us, blinds us, and keeps us from hearing from God or obeying when He speaks. I've seen too many examples of fear keeping people from enjoying fulfilling human relationships, from taking significant steps in their careers, and, worst of all, from being used effectively for the kingdom of God.

In the margin describe the "course" you believe God has given you to run. Then state what is holding you back from "running" this course.

Too many of us avoid or run from the prospects that frighten us. Fearing rejection, we avoid close contact with other people. Fearing failure, we simply stop trying to accomplish anything. And fearing people, we keep our mouths shut when we should be talking to friends, coworkers, and neighbors about all that God has done for us.

On the scale below, rate how often fear forces you off the course God has given you.

Often   **Seldom**

When we run from the things that frighten us, we've handed Satan the victory in a gift-wrapped box with a bow on top. We've essentially waved the white flag and said to the Devil, "You win!" Our paralysis in the face of fear gives victory to an enemy who loves nothing more than to freeze us in our tracks, to cripple us, and to render us useless for God's kingdom.

In what ways can you identify the fingerprint of Satan on some of your fears?

_____

FACING YOUR FEARS

Death will always be death, sickness will always be sickness, and failure will always be failure. And when we refuse to confront our fears over those things, we choose to walk in darkness and to avoid reality.

When we are fearful, no matter what may be causing our fear, it's important for us to be honest with ourselves and with God about what's really scaring us. Trying to appear strong and fearless on the outside while we're in complete turmoil on the inside gets us nowhere.

Where in your life do you feel like you play the game of trying to appear strong but internally feel scared?

_____

Psalm 34 is probably my favorite Bible passage on dealing honestly with fear. In this psalm, David tells us how he handled the multitude of fears that confronted him during the many colorful chapters of his walk with the Lord.

Open your Bible and copy the words to Psalm 34:4 into the space below.

David didn't deny being afraid. He didn't slap a happy face over that which truly frightened him or live in denial, insisting that "everything is just fine" when it really wasn't. Instead of denying the fear in his life, he did something with it. He took it to the one place where we can all receive comfort when we're afraid—to God Himself!

How can Psalm 34:4 help you face your fears?

_____

Where do you need this Scripture's truth applied in your life? _____

Don't run from or deny your fears. That's dishonest and only makes things worse.

Don't run from your fears. You *will* have to face them one day, and you can never grow in your faith until you do.

God cares when we are afraid, and He has given us a way to confront and defeat our fears. It's by exposing them to the light He gives us through His Son, Jesus Christ.

In the margin write a one- or two-sentence prayer that properly communicates to God your fears.

day *Five*

Fear's Strong Antidote

More than 360 times in the Bible we read variations of God telling us not to be afraid. And time after time we see Jesus personally demonstrating what it takes to live lives under God's control and not under the control of fear.

One of the many things Jesus came to deliver us from was fear, but far too many believers still allow their fears—real, rational fears as well as fears they've cooked up in their own minds—to control them. But why are so many believers absolutely crippled by these anxieties? I believe it's because too many of us are dealing with them from positions of darkness, and not from the position of walking in the light of Jesus Christ.

This is what Jesus was talking about when He said, "If anyone walks in the night, he stumbles, because the light is not in him" (John 11:10).

Hard as it may be to feel your way from one dark room to another without running into something or hurting yourself, it's just as difficult to work your way through a season of fear without using the right standards—the ones God has given us in His Word. Self-talk and gritting your teeth really aren't much help in the grip of paralyzing fear and constant worry. Even counseling, worthy as that might be at times, won't help you when you face life-crippling fears sent by the enemy of your soul.

The only thing that will ultimately defeat your fears once and for all is your focus on and application of the truth of God's Word in your daily life.

On the scale below, rate your level of focus regarding God's Word.

Very Little   **Daily**

What is one way you will improve your focus? _____

THE GREATEST FEAR

While there are many things we might fear, most people will tell you that they fear death more than anything else. In some respects, the fear of death is natural and healthy; it's the "self-preservation" instinct God has given us so that we don't take our lives lightly and unnecessarily put ourselves in danger.

On the scale below rate how often you think you apply the truth of God's Word.

Very Little   **Daily**

What is one way you will improve your level of application? _____

While the Bible doesn't downplay or deny the pain we feel when a loved one dies or when we face death ourselves, it does tell us that death is not the end of those who believe in Jesus Christ. Our Lord personally defeated death once and for all through His death on the cross and His resurrection three days later.

As children of Adam and Eve, members of a fallen race, each of us must face that final enemy one day, no matter how consistently we work out, eat right, and shun harmful habits. As someone once said, "The one thing we know for certain about life is this: No one gets out of it alive!"

But even there, even in that "valley of the shadow" that all of us must enter one day, we walk in the radiant, encircling, enveloping light of the Lord Jesus Christ. *And where He leads us, He will keep us.* We can walk in the daylight of His comforting presence right up until that moment when we step into eternal daylight—and see Him face to face.

How does death inevitably affect the way you live your life? _____

How can Jesus transform our fear concerning death into something positive? _____

Jesus understood that His men were afraid of the deadly dangers they faced in Judea. And He cared, taking the time to teach them some principles on how to face and defeat their fears.

He does the same for us today as He allows us—even *encourages* us—to take our fears to Him. Shining the light of His infinite goodness and grace on every dark corner of our lives, He helps us put those fears in their place—*behind us.*

List one fear that you want God to "put behind" you today. _____

Then ask God to put that fear behind you. He will do it!

Before the Session

1. Ask learners to bring something to class that represents a time when they put themselves in a careless situation. [For example, a learner could bring a photo of a river-rafting trip.] Use these items in During the Session Step 1 below.
2. Bring a flashlight to class. [See During the Session Step 4 below.]

During the Session

1. Once your class has gathered, allow learners to share what they brought that reflects a careless situation they once put themselves in. *Ask: How much control do we have as far as whether or not to place ourselves in careless situations? Is it a general rule that we should always avoid careless situations?* Allow time for discussion. Read John 11:7-11 aloud. Ask: *How does our faith sometimes place us in careless situations?* Allow time for discussion. As a follow-up discussion, ask learners to share how they responded to the last interactive of Day 1 on page 18.
2. Read aloud again John 11:9-10. Ask: *What do you think Jesus meant by this? What does the Day 2 material reveal about the specific hostility Jesus was facing if He went to Jerusalem?* Emphasize that Jesus genuinely faced some grave threats if He went to Jerusalem. Yet He didn't want to miss out on showing His disciples the glory of God. Ask learners to share their responses to the three interactive questions at the end of Day 2 on pages 19-20.
3. Remind learners of the description of roads in the ancient Roman Empire. Use the Day 3 material for further explanation. Next, if possible, turn the lights off in your classroom space. Allow learners to soak in the feeling of sitting in the dark. While the lights are off, emphasize that light, the way Jesus utilized the image, referred to God's Word—namely God's revelation to His people. Explain that the darkness symbolized evil and confusion. Ask: *How does sitting in the dark, right now, remind us of the dangers associated with doing that which is evil?* Allow time for discussion. For follow-up, allow learners to share what they listed in the chart on page 21 under Day 3.

To the Leader:

So often our difficult circumstances are woven together with a sense of fear. This session outlines how Jesus modeled a sense of no fear when seeking to do what was right. Following God requires courage. When it comes to our faith, we may not face death but we do face other pressures. As you pray and prepare for this lesson, ask God to help learners face their fears when it comes to living out their faith in the world.

4. Pull out the flashlight and turn it on. Say: *Walking in the dark is unnerving, but walking with some light makes all the difference. Jesus gives us light to see in this world.* Allow learners to share how they responded to the remaining interactives of Day 3 on pages 21-22.

5. Based on the first interactive of Day 4 on page 22, allow learners to share the "course" they think God has called them to take in life. Ask: *How often does fear knock you off your course?* [Use the second interactive of Day 4 on p. 22 for reference.] Discuss learners responses to the interactive on the middle of page 23 in Day 4. Emphasize our desire to be strong or at least make people *think* we are strong. Discuss why this seems to be important to us.

6. Ask a volunteer to read aloud Psalm 34:4. Ask learners to share how they think this one verse can help them face their fears. [Utilize the interactives on the top of page 24 for reference.] Say: *Sometimes it is hard to take God's Word at face value because we are so doubtful.* Ask: *How have you successfully allowed Scriptures such as Psalm 34:4 to affect the way you face life?* Ask learners to share their responses.

7. Say: *We mustn't forget how important it is for us to believe what God promised.* Jesus asked His disciples to trust Him. In the same way, God asks us to trust Him. Ask learners to share how they responded to the first three interactives of Day 5 on pages 25-26. Ask: *What is one fear that you want God to "put behind" you today?* [Refer to the final interactive of Day 5 on page 26.]

8. Close in prayer, asking God to begin to work His promises in the lives of the learners. Assure learners that what God has promised, He will do!

God, Do You Really Care ... When I'm Hurting?

The Hurt of Hurts

There may be no greater pain on earth than that which comes with the death of a loved one. Yes, there are plenty of other hurts to go around. We ache over bruised or broken relationships. We grieve over unfulfilled goals and dreams and countless other disappointments in life. But death—be it the death of parent, sibling, spouse, child, or dear friend—hurts even more profoundly, mostly because it's so final.

You would think it would be different for those of us who rest in the hope of heaven—who know our saved loved one is in a far, far better place. And it is. As the Scripture says, don't "grieve as do the rest who have no hope" (1 Thess. 4:13). But it still hurts. Our loved one may be in heaven, but we aren't. We're still on this side of eternity, with all its loneliness, sorrows, and pain. And when someone we love so much slips away to the other side, we miss that person terribly. We know we'll never see that individual again in this life.

How has the death of a loved one affected you?

_____

John's account of the story of Lazarus of Bethany gives us examples of how so many of us might respond when we lose someone near and dear to us. As Jesus arrived in Bethany, His dear friends Mary and Martha were obviously rocked with pain and fresh grief over the loss of their brother.

What made it so much worse was that it was a loss they believed would never happen! The Lord Himself had sent them a message that their brother's sickness wouldn't end in death.

It's one thing to try to absorb the enormous shock of losing our loved one, but it's a whole other level of pain when we feel so sure we'd heard the voice of God telling us that things would turn out all right—that our loved one wouldn't die.

In the margin, describe a time when you were certain God was going to "come through" for you but it didn't happen the way you thought.

By the time Jesus finally arrived in town, Lazarus had been in the tomb for four days. To the grieving sisters, this late arrival must have seemed like a broken promise—and like one big contradiction.

Read John 11:17-20. In the space below, list all the people mentioned in these verses. Then indicate how these people were reacting to the loss of Lazarus.

Lazarus was dead. And what's worse, Jesus had let them down. The pain must have been unbearable.

In lesson 1, I pointed out that God doesn't always come immediately to the rescue when we're in a time of need but that He always sends us a personal word. But what do we do when it seems that the word we have received contradicts the reality in our lives? When it seems that God has failed to keep a personal promise? When it seems that this God who identifies Himself as the personification of love and compassion has contradicted Himself and let us down?

As odd as it may sound—and as difficult as it may be to do when we are suffering—those are the very times when we need to focus on our God and His love for us more than ever. Why? Because it may well be that He's about to do something for us beyond all our expectations. After pleading with Him for an A or B—or possibly C—He comes walking in through the back door with Z. And we say, "I could have never imagined or predicted *that!*"

When God doesn't seem to "come through" for us, how should we express our faith in the midst of the confusion?

Why the Delay?

Although it's hard for us to grasp in this era of cell phones, pagers, and instant messaging, it's highly possible that Lazarus had already died by the time Jesus received word of his illness. Perea was about 30 miles from Bethany, and it wasn't until two days had passed that Jesus and the disciples began their journey back to Bethany. By the time they arrived, Mary and Martha already considered the situation closed. Lazarus was gone. Jesus hadn't come. Life had to go on.

What's important in this story, however, isn't the timing of Lazarus's death or of Jesus' arrival in Bethany, but the intention behind Jesus' delayed response. As we read this account, what jumps out at us is that Jesus had a purpose for His delay.

He always does.

Mary and Martha had put out a first-century 911 call. It was an emergency needing attention *right now,* or "STAT," as they say in the emergency room. The sisters knew their brother would die if something wasn't done, and they did the one thing they knew beyond any doubt could help him—they called for Jesus.

But Jesus didn't just drop everything and head for Bethany. Instead, He sent the sisters a message of comfort and assurance, then stayed put for two more days. By the time He left Perea, Lazarus was certainly dead. But that, it turns out, was part of God's plan for the glorification of the Son.

**Why do you think God sometimes waits rather
than acts quickly when it comes to our struggles?**

_____

_____

**How can John 11:4-6 help us understand God's
reasons for waiting?**

_____

_____

This is not a case of someone being caught off guard or miscalculating the situation. This was an example of a Savior who cares deeply when His people are hurting, but who has a plan to teach us and expand our faith in the very midst of our pain.

SAME PAIN, DIFFERENT EXPRESSIONS

As you read of Mary and Martha in the Gospels, it becomes fairly obvious that these two women—while they both had tremendous faith in and love for Jesus—were "wired" very differently. That is evident in how they responded to Jesus when He finally arrived at the outskirts of Bethany: "Martha therefore, when she heard that Jesus was coming, went to meet Him, but Mary stayed at the house" (John 11:20).

There are some Bible verses I read and immediately understand what God is saying to me through them. But there are others I can *feel*. John 11:20 is one of the latter. When I read it, I can just *feel* Mary's disappointment over the death of her brother. But I can also feel her disappointment with Jesus Himself. Mary had believed with all her heart that her brother wouldn't die and that Jesus would show up in time to heal him. Now, with her brother in the grave four days, she couldn't even summon what it took to go outside her house and face the dearest person in her life.

Have you ever felt that way toward God? Have you ever wanted to say to Him, "If You had only stepped in sooner, then I wouldn't be feeling this pain"? Have you ever felt as though God let you down and abandoned you when you needed Him most? Worse yet, have you ever believed that you heard a personal word from God—a Bible-confirmed message just to you—only to find that what you believed you heard didn't come to pass?

Which of the above questions relates closest to your own story? _____

How would you answer any or all of the questions listed in the above paragraph? _____

That was what Mary grappled with as Jesus arrived in Bethany. But we will see as we continue on in this story that Jesus cares when we are hurting, even when—maybe *especially* when—we are in such pain that we can't even approach Him to talk about it.

Pain and a Personal Word

In lesson 1 we talked about God's kindness and care in sending us a personal word in our times of sickness and distress—a message just for us through the Holy Spirit's illumination of His written Word.

We need to remember that when God sends us a personal word, we can count on Him to keep it. And He keeps His word to us when He comes to us personally and shows us how much He cares as He ministers to us in our pain.

He may not show up when we expect Him to.

He may not show up in the way we expect Him to.

But He will always show up on time … not our time, maybe, but the right time.

Is it easy for you to count on others ? Why or why not? _____

Has anyone been a disappointment to you when it comes to keeping his or her word? _____

Jesus demonstrated this principle in Mary and Martha's situation. Though at first He ministered to them through a word only, it was just a matter of timing as to when He would arrive on the scene and tend to His dear friends' situation in a tangible and personal way.

When Jesus first arrived near Bethany, the first thing Martha and Mary did was register a complaint: "Lord, if You had been here, my brother would not have died" (John 11:21,32). The way I read this, it wasn't just a complaint, it was also an accusation. In effect, they were saying, "Our brother wouldn't be dead now if You had just come when we called You!"

How honest are you when it comes to expressing your feelings and emotions toward God? _____

The fact that Martha and Mary both registered the same complaint with Jesus tells me that in the four days prior to Jesus' arrival in Bethany—the same four days their brother had been wrapped in a shroud and sealed in a tomb—they had been talking about their feelings with one another. Hurt and anger had to have been part of that conversation.

But what stands out to me most in this scene isn't Mary and Martha's complaints. They were just doing what so many believers do when they're in pain—blame God. ("If He's such a loving God, how could He allow me to suffer so much?") What really strikes me about this scene is Jesus' response.

Silence.

In my own human thinking, it's easy for me to imagine Jesus listening to Mary and Martha's accusations, then sternly rebuking and correcting the two women. I can just hear Him saying, "Just who do you think you're talking to? Don't you know who I am? I am God's chosen One, and I have prerogatives of where to go and when to go there."

Yet Jesus didn't respond directly to these complaints. He didn't chide or correct them but simply went about comforting them … and preparing them for the miracle He was about to do on their behalf.

But why didn't Jesus correct Mary and Martha? I believe it was because He knew what was really in their hearts.

An understanding friend knows our hearts. He or she knows that when we're hurting, we may say things we might not otherwise say. A friend like that is able to see through our words into our pain and feel that pain with us.

Identify someone in your life who has felt your pain.

How was that person sympathetic toward you?

I believe that's what was happening as Jesus listened to Mary and Martha expressing their disappointment. Jesus knew these women loved Him dearly. He knew that their words weren't coming from what was really in their hearts toward Him.

It was just their grief talking.

How did Jesus' actions in John 11:17-32 reveal the heart of God?

_____

_____

Jesus Responds

Arriving near Bethany, Jesus was greeted by a scene of incredible hurt and disappointment. Both Martha and Mary were hurting and angry, and they were joined in their grieving by what was probably a sizeable group of Jews who had come to mourn with them. Eventually (and I'll get to this in more detail later) Mary came out of her home to see Jesus, and the first thing she did was fall at His feet, weeping.

And what was Jesus' response to all the pain and grieving? John tells us, "When Jesus therefore saw her weeping, and the Jews who came with her also weeping, He was deeply moved in spirit, *and was troubled*" (John 11:33, emphasis mine).

We can easily understand the "moved in spirit" part. When Jesus saw and felt the huge wave of pain and sorrow rolling out from that scene, it moved Him. Yes, Jesus was the Son of God, but He was also a man who felt the same kinds of emotions we feel. There was no way He could be at a scene like this and not be emotionally touched.

But there was something more here.

Jesus wasn't just moved in spirit but also "troubled." In the original language, the word *troubled* can also be read as "disturbed" or "shaken," suggesting that Jesus was seeing something beyond the grief and tears.

With His heart still troubled and disturbed, Jesus asked the mourners where Lazarus was buried. As they all made their way toward the tomb, the people could easily see that Jesus was touched by what was going on around Him, and verse 35 tells us why: "Jesus wept."

Think back on your own personal losses and tragedies. How did you typically believe God was reacting?

_____ **He was stoic**

_____ **He didn't care.**

_____ **He was weeping.**

_____ **Other:** _____

How does John 11:35 change the way you understand God's capacity to grieve?

\
_____

When the Jewish mourners saw Jesus crying, many of them naturally assumed it was for the same reason everyone else was weeping—because He loved Lazarus and was grieving over his death. But this was much more than weeping over the loss of a friend.

Others at the gravesite saw something else in Jesus' tears. John tells us: "But some of them said, 'Could not this man, who opened the eyes of the blind man, have kept this man also from dying?' " (11:37). In other words, some might have believed Jesus was crying because He was helpless—because there was nothing He could do for a man already dead. And Jesus wouldn't have missed the implication of their words: If He couldn't keep Lazarus from dying in the first place, then maybe He's not everything people say He is.

What do Jesus' tears mean to you? _____

Over the centuries people have attempted to explain the reason for Jesus' tears in this scene. Some have held that He was moved in spirit and weeping simply because He so deeply sympathized with the grief of those around Him. That theory has some merit … but there's another explanation we need to consider.

Throughout His ministry, Jesus had never responded this way in the face of human suffering and grief. Although Jesus had already been at several scenes of death, unspeakable suffering, and deeply felt pain, His response had not been to cry but to roll up His sleeves to heal and raise the dead.

While I firmly believe that Jesus was moved with emotion because of what was happening in the lives of these two women, I believe His tears were also motivated by something else, something no one—not Mary, not Martha, and not the mourners who had come to comfort them—could comprehend but Jesus Himself.

day Five

A Different Kind of Grief

The Gospels record two instances of Jesus weeping—outside Lazarus's tomb and as He looked out over the holy city of Jerusalem and wept over its lack of faith: "O Jerusalem, Jerusalem, you who kill the prophets and stone those sent to you, how often I have longed to gather your children together, as a hen gathers her chicks under her wings, but you were not willing" (Matt. 23:37, NIV).

This was Jesus crying tears of grief, but not because He was mourning over the loss of a loved one. These were tears over a people who had turned their backs on God, who refused to receive what He had long ago promised and offered to them. Jesus was grieved to His very core for one reason: The people of Israel were rejecting God's chosen One.

I believe His tears in the scene outside Lazarus's grave were motivated in part by the very same feelings.

Open your Bible and copy John 11:38-40 in the margin.

As the moment approached for Jesus to bring Lazarus back from the dead, He gave the command to have the stone rolled away from the grave. Again, a grieving Martha protested, pointing out the obvious: "Lord, by this time there will be a stench, for he has been dead four days" (John 11:39).

Martha, though she had already had a very intense spiritual conversation with Jesus just outside of town, was still thinking in the natural. She still hadn't reconciled her brother's death with the Lord's promise that his illness would not end in death. It had ended in death! How could you get around it?

When we read Jesus' response to Martha, He sounds more than a little peeved that she doesn't understand that something miraculous and spectacular is about to happen. "Did I not say," Jesus told her, "if you believe, you will see the glory of God?" (v. 40). When I read, "Did I not say...?" I can't help but think of a good scolding along the lines of, "How many times do I have to tell you?" or "If you'd just pay attention, you'd know that."

I believed Jesus was disturbed and troubled at the grief and crying on the scene not just because of the natural human emotions but because the tears of grief weren't mixed with tears of faith. He saw people that day who were so controlled by their circumstances that they couldn't grasp what He already had told them—that God would be glorified that day! In other words, they were focused on what had caused their pain—the death of Lazarus—and not on the One who had come to defeat death for Lazarus and his sisters that day … and for the rest of us when He gave Himself up to die for our sins.

Do you agree with Dr. Evans's conclusion about Jesus' tears? Why or why not?

_____

There's nothing at all wrong with us allowing ourselves to feel pain when we lose a loved one—or for any number of other reasons. In fact, I would say there is something wrong with us if we don't. But when we know Jesus Christ and know that He cares and will be there for us in the midst of our pain, there will be an element of trust and joy in our tears. We know that Jesus Christ will keep every promise He has ever made.

How has this lesson affected the way you understand the way Jesus grieves when we go through loss and pain? _____

How can faith in Christ change the way we grieve in this world?

_____

Before the Session

1. Be prepared to share about your own sense of loss. If you are sharing about someone you have lost, bring a picture or something that reflects the essence of how meaningful this person was to you.
2. Pray for sensitivity as you lead your class in exploring the painful experiences they have faced.

During the Session

1. Open your class time by sharing your own story of loss. Say: *Today we are discussing how God meets us in the midst of our pain. I would like to share my own story of loss.* Present your prepared story. After sharing, allow learners time to share how they responded to the first interactive of Day 1 on page 29. Ask: *What type of conversations did you have with God when you were in the process of losing someone you loved?* Ask a volunteer to read aloud John 11:17-20. Ask learners to imagine how the people described in these verses were reacting to the loss of Lazarus. Ask learners to share how they responded to the final interactive of Day 1 on page 30.
2. Refer to the first interactive of Day 2 on page 31. Ask the question listed in this interactive: *Why do you think God sometimes waits rather than acts quickly when it comes to our struggles?* Then ask, *How can John 11:4-6 help us understand God's reasons for waiting?* Explain that one of the hardest things we face is the reality of not understanding God's actions. Ask learners to share how they reacted to the last interactives of Day 2 on page 32. Be sure to affirm that being honest with God is OK.
3. Ask a volunteer to read aloud John 11:21-32. Ask: *How many times can you identify disappointment in these verses, as well as in verses 17-20? Do you think folks felt let down by God? Who specifically do you think felt let down?* Follow up with asking learners to share how they responded to the first interactives of Day 3 on page 33.
4. Ask: *What can we learn from the fact that Jesus simply listened to the grieving sisters Mary and Martha? Why do you think He didn't feel a need to correct them?* Explain that Jesus models compassion and understand-

To the Leader:

No doubt folks in your class are hurting in some way or another. Week 3 of Tony Evans's material addresses the nexus where God meets us in the midst of our hurts. Pray for openness about the things people are struggling with. Be prepared to share your own stories of loss in order to demonstrate transparency with your class or small group.

ing for grieving hearts. Refer to the final interactives of Day 3 on the bottom of page 34 and the top of page 35. Allow learners time to share their responses.

5. Ask learners to share how they responded to the first interactive of Day 4 on page 36. Ask: *What does it mean to you when the Scripture says: "Jesus wept" (John 11:35)?* Explain that some people were amazed at Jesus' tears. At the same time, some thought His tears were a sign of His failure to be able to help Lazarus. Ask: *What do Jesus' tears mean to you?* [Refer to the last interactive of Day 4 on p. 36.]

6. Ask a volunteer to read aloud John 11:38-40. Ask: *What do these verses reveal about Jesus' grief over Lazarus's death?* Say: *In the material for Day 5, Dr. Evans presented a different perspective regarding Jesus' tears. Do you agree with his conclusion? Why or why not?* [See first interactive of Day 5 on the middle of p. 38.]

7. Conclude this lesson by allowing learners to share how they responded to the last interactives of Day 5 on page 38.

God, Do You Really Care ...When I'm Disappointed?

day One

Jesus, Where Were You?

Is disappointment losing something good you expected or experiencing something bad you didn't expect at all? It may be a little of both. Either way, it hurts.

Taking it a step further, we might say that disappointment is the pain we experience when something we've been holding on to dies. It could be the death of a loved one, but it could also be the death of a vision, the death of a dream, or the death of our hopes for the fulfillment of a promise.

What types of "death" have you experienced around your life? _____

I think it's safe to say that every believer has had something die in his or her life and felt the devastating letdown that follows. And in the wake of such crushing disappointment, we find ourselves asking, *God, where were You in all this?*

In the margin write the name of someone you know who has asked the above question. Then describe the circumstances that led to the asking of this question.

That's a query common to all humankind, and it's the very question both Martha and Mary asked Jesus when He finally arrived near the village of Bethany ... four days after the death of their brother Lazarus.

When Jesus finally arrived in Bethany, disappointment hung in the air like L.A. smog. John tells us that a crowd of Jewish people had made the two-mile trek from Jerusalem to Bethany to console and comfort Mary and Martha.

Into the midst of all this wailing and tears came Jesus.

Yes, the Master had arrived. But too late to help.

Or so they thought.

Losing their brother when Jesus had distinctly said that his sickness would *not* end in death was a devastating blow for Mary and Martha. The sisters' responses to Jesus revealed the disappointment that permeated their grief.

When Martha heard that Jesus was nearing Bethany, she ran out to meet Him. "Lord," she said, "if You had been here my brother would not have died" (John 11:21). Mary said the same thing a few minutes later.

Those who are disappointed and hurting often use "If only" statements. "*If only* I had …" or "*If only* he had …" or "*If only* it hadn't happened this way…." Statements such as these reflect the belief that if someone had made another choice or turned another way, or if circumstances had taken a turn to the left instead of the right, then a particular situation would have turned out differently.

Both of these women wanted an answer to one simple question: *Where had Jesus been when they needed Him?* They knew that their brother had been deathly sick and that they had called out to Jesus for help. But the hours and days slipped by, Jesus never showed up, and Lazarus drew his last rattling breath, and died.

In the margin, list some contemporary issues that make us wonder where God is.

Jesus had waited two more days in Perea before coming to see them. That hurt! The two women had deep disappointment that hovered on the edge of being *bitter* disappointment.

When Mary and Martha said to Jesus, "If You had been here, my brother would not have died," what they were really saying was, "This is Your fault, Jesus, because we called You knowing that You could have kept Lazarus alive, but You did nothing to help us."

Those of us who have been through a situation where we felt bitter disappointment know that this is a time when our true feelings tend to rise to the surface. In times like these, we're less likely to weigh our words. We're hurting, and the hurt sometimes comes pouring out of our mouths.

There is a touch of anger in Martha and Mary's words—and maybe a little bitterness as well. They both got right at the heart of what they were feeling that day, and it wasn't pretty. In essence, they were telling Jesus that He had let them down—at the very time when they needed Him so desperately.

As I pointed out earlier, Mary and Martha weren't the only ones to voice their disappointment. Some of the Jewish people who had come to comfort and console them—probably including some of Jesus' enemies—expressed their own cynical brand of disappointment: "Could not this man, who opened the eyes of the blind man, have kept this man also from dying?" (v. 37).

But there was a profound difference between the way Mary and Martha expressed their disappointment and the way some of the mourners did.

In the margin indicate how you think Mary and Martha's disappointment was different from that of the other mourners.

day *Two*

Where to Bring Your Disappointment

Do you believe that disappointment—even bitter disappointment—and faith can exist in the same heart? Can the two commingle? Can they produce blessings such as a strengthened faith and deeper relationship with God?

What do you think? Can disappointment and faith coexist? Explain your response in the margin.

Sounds like a bit of a stretch, doesn't it?

In fact, disappointment and faith might coexist better than you would have imagined.

Do you believe that God is OK with your expressions of disappointment? Does He care enough when you are disappointed to listen to you, speak to you, gently reason with you, and comfort you as you pour out your pain-filled heart before Him? Or is it better to keep your disappointment to yourself—sealed up tightly inside a smooth religious veneer?

Record in the margin how the idea of expressing your disappointment toward God makes you feel.

Obviously Martha was disappointed—disappointed that their little family had been torn apart by death and disappointed with their Friend, Jesus. But we need to take note of where she took those feelings—to Jesus Himself! There were plenty of mourners around that week who would have sympathized with her and shared their own doubts and disappointments about Jesus. But she didn't go to those people. She just took it all to Jesus, laying it at His feet.

Martha's words reflect both her disappointment and her faith in Jesus and the Father. In one breath she said, "If You had been here, my brother would not have died," but in the very next breath she acknowledged, "Even now I know that whatever You ask of God, God will give You" (v. 22).

While Martha was disappointed with Jesus—as well as angry and maybe even bitter—she went straight to Him simply because she knew who He really was.

Even as Martha spilled out her heart, telling the Lord how let down she felt, she also affirmed her faith in Jesus. The mourners noted Jesus' arrival too. But they voiced their grief in a completely different way, basically questioning whether Jesus was all He had claimed to be.

And how did Jesus react?

He responded to Martha's disappointment by conversing with her, giving her comfort and assurance, and leading her into a deeper faith in Him. Conversely, He had nothing to say to those on the scene that doubted Him and questioned His credentials.

When your faith is firmly in Jesus Christ, you don't need to hide your anger, hurt, or disappointment from Him. After all, He knows what you're thinking and feeling anyway, and He will never reject you for pouring out those emotions percolating in your soul.

Who or what contributes to our sense of feeling that we are not allowed to share our gut-level feeling with God? _____

Part of life on this earth is going through disappointments. Sometimes the disappointment and pain over our losses can be so deep and so consuming that we can't help but cry out to God and ask Him if He really cares. But even at our lowest points in life, we can be assured of two things.

First, we can be assured that God cares when we are disappointed. He loves us with a love far wider and deeper than anything we can imagine, and when we are hurting, He feels it with us and seeks to comfort us. The psalmist tells us: "The LORD is near to the brokenhearted and saves those who are crushed in spirit" (Ps. 34:18).

But there is a second assurance in this story. As we communicate with Him honestly and openly about our disappointments, telling Him our sorrow and despair, we can be assured that we love and serve a Savior who has the Father's ear. And He's a Father who will give Jesus anything He asks for.

Martha demonstrated that kind of faith, and before this scene was over, Jesus would give her what she had asked for in the first place—even if it didn't happen in the way she had expected. He would give her something infinitely more amazing than a healing for her brother. He would give her a resurrection.

Based on Day 2's material, list in the margin at least two reasons why we ought to share honestly with God.

day Three

Resting in the Faith of Another

Martha had told Jesus, "I know that whatever You ask of God, God will give You." In saying that, she was not only acknowledging who Jesus was and who God was but also the perfect relationship between them.

The Father and the Son have always lived in perfect relationship. While Jesus ministered on earth, He was completely committed to doing the will of the Father and *only* the will of the Father. At the same time, the Father was committed to the authority He had given the Son—to do and say the things God wanted us to see and hear.

Martha grasped this perfect Father-Son relationship, and she understood that in her time of deep disappointment—a time when her faith could very well have been shaken to its core—she could go to Jesus and "piggy-back" on *His* perfect faith. She knew that Jesus was in perfect harmony with His Father and that nothing He asked for would ever be turned down from above.

If that seems like a stretch or like I'm reading more into this account than what God really has to say, then note what the apostle Paul declared concerning this aspect of faith: "This was in accordance with the eternal purpose which He carried out in Christ Jesus our Lord, in whom we have boldness and confident access *through faith in Him*" (Eph. 3:11–12).

When Martha acknowledged Jesus' identity and His relationship with the Father, she began with the phrase *I know.* Martha was in a situation where she was sure of very little ... except Jesus' relationship with the Father. The only thing she really knew for sure was that her brother was dead and that there was nothing she could do to change that fact. But as Martha looked outside her present situation, if only for a moment, she was able to state with absolute confidence who Jesus was and what the Father would do for Him.

Concerning the identity of Christ, what "I know" statements can you list in the margin?

How do these statements affect the way you work through challenges? _____

Most believers in our culture end their prayers with words such as, "In Jesus' name, Amen." But what does it mean to pray in Jesus' name? This has to be more than just a nice-sounding tagline to our prayers to make them "extra religious."

When we pray "in Jesus' name," we are actually claiming the authority of Jesus Christ Himself in our prayers. We're applying the same kind of "I know" faith Martha showed when she acknowledged Jesus' relationship with the Father. When we pray about our disappointment and pain in our Lord's name, we are essentially saying to Him, "I need You to back me up on this, Jesus, because I'm not sure I'm getting through. I'm too frustrated, too angry, too weak, too broken, and too confused to know if my prayers are making it past the ceiling. But I know above all this that the Father will never turn You down."

In the midst of what might have been the darkest time of her life, Martha appealed to what she knew to be true—that Jesus was the Son of God and that the Father gave Him what He requested. Because of that, she knew deep in her heart that her situation and her circumstances wouldn't have the final word that day. She couldn't know for sure what Jesus would ask for, but she knew that whatever it was, God would do it for Him ... and for her.

Based on Martha's claim in John 11:22, what claim can we make concerning the struggles we face?

day Four

Jesus Gets the Last Word

In the grip of grief and perplexity, Martha was somehow able to acknowledge Jesus' identity and His perfect relationship with the Father. As a result, she received yet another personal word from the lips of God's Son. And this time, it was face to face.

"Your brother will rise again" (John 11:23, emphasis mine).

Martha knew her Scripture. Looking up into the Lord's face, she responded, "I know that he will rise again in the resurrection on the last day."

Most Jews—excluding the unhappy Sadducee party—believed in an end-times resurrection. The Pharisees, the dominant sect in the Jewish religious leadership at that time, believed in and taught the scriptural fact of the resurrection. Jewish boys of the time were required to undergo years of Bible teaching and study. Although Martha had probably not undergone that kind of study, she was aware of the teaching of the end-time resurrection and understood that her brother—as well as all other believers—would one day be raised from the dead.

Taken by itself, Jesus' promise that Lazarus would rise again could have been heard as a strong word of encouragement in the midst of Martha's struggle. It would be much like a modern-day believer telling a brother or sister in Christ that his or her saved friend or loved one is now "in a better place," specifically in the presence of the Lord. That's a wonderful truth, and there's no denying it. It's a fact that can make all the difference to a grieving believer mourning the loss of a loved one.

But Jesus had something even more for Martha that day.

IT'S *WHO* YOU KNOW

Jesus didn't correct Martha when she acknowledged the final resurrection. After all, she was speaking biblical truth! Instead, He took her a step further in her faith, telling her, "I am the resurrection and the life; he who believes in Me will live even if he dies, and everyone who lives and believes in Me will never die. Do you believe this?" (vv. 25–26).

In the margin write what John 11:25-26 means to you and how this statement impacts your life.

Martha already had gone partway to where Jesus wanted to take her. She already had spoken sound and right doctrine when she acknowledged that there would be a resurrection for all believers at the end of time. But Jesus wanted to draw a distinction for Martha—and for us—between doctrine and the *person* of Jesus Christ. In essence, Jesus was telling her that her belief in the resurrection was a sound and right one but that *He* is the resurrection. The reason her brother would rise from the dead was because *He* had said so.

Of course, sound biblical teaching holds a vital place in the life of every believer. We've got to know *what* we believe and *why* we believe it. But as important as solid teaching is, we can't get so stuck on it that we miss the person of Jesus Christ. If we remain stuck on knowing doctrine without knowing Jesus as the personification of all truth, we won't be prepared for those inevitable times in life when the roof falls in and the ground shakes beneath our feet. But when we acknowledge who He really is, we will receive the comfort and blessings we seek.

Why is belief so essential for experiencing God's blessing? _____

But there is a condition to that, and it's this: Our confession has to be verbal. We'll look at this tomorrow.

day Five

"Do You Believe This?"

It was a pointed question, and it needed a direct answer.

Looking steadily into Martha's tear-stained face, Jesus had said, "I am the resurrection and the life; he who believes in Me will live even if he dies, and everyone who lives and believes in Me will never die."

Those were the facts. And Jesus wanted Martha to respond to those facts.

"Do you believe this?"

The answer had to be yes or no.

Everything was in place for Jesus to perform an awesome miracle. But before that physical miracle of raising Lazarus from the dead would take place, Jesus wanted to do an inner miracle in the heart of His friend Martha. He wanted to see her move forward from mere book and head knowledge to a more personal, living faith.

"Do you believe this?"

When Jesus asked Martha if she believed He was the resurrection and that everyone who believes in Him would live forever, it wasn't just rhetorical. He expected an answer. He wanted Martha to verbalize what she believed, not to be silent about it.

And Martha did respond.

Without missing a beat, she replied, "Yes, Lord; I have believed that You are the Christ, the Son of God, even He who comes into the world" (v. 27).

The real key to any kind of blessing from God is to verbally acknowledge who Jesus Christ really is—the Son of God, the all-powerful Second Person of the Trinity. And when we are disappointed and hurting,

> "The real key to any kind of blessing from God is to verbally acknowledge who Jesus Christ really is—the Son of God, the all-powerful Second Person of the Trinity."—Tony Evans

we have an opportunity to experience a "right now" kind of God, not just a God who blesses us in "the sweet by-and-by." But in order to receive a blessing from Him, we must be willing to acknowledge Him—not just in our heads, not just in our hearts, but with our mouths.

Martha wasn't going to get her miracle that day until she was able to verbally acknowledge Jesus' relationship with the Father and His true identity.

In the margin, indicate what people say about Jesus today. Then in one sentence write out the way you describe Jesus to people.

When we are hurting and disappointed, when something has died in our lives and left us feeling as though our world is falling apart, *our first response to Jesus should be to acknowledge who He really is.* My friend, there is power in declaring who He is and what He has done and can do. Who is He? He is the one and only Son of God who receives anything and everything He requests of the Father. When we acknowledge that, He is free to comfort us in our pain and give us perspective in our disappointments.

Why is knowing the identity of Jesus so critical?

_____

How does this practically apply to your life?_____

_____

And more than that—He'll perform a resurrection.

Jesus knew Martha and Mary were disappointed—bitterly so. He also knew they had much to learn in the midst of their disappointment. Though they didn't realize it in the turmoil of their sorrow, He had a plan to turn their disappointment into praise.

This is a God who cares when we are disappointed ... even when the disappointment is in Him.

leader Guide

NOTES

Before the Session

Take a piece of cardboard and cut it into the shape of a tombstone. Use this for the During the Session Step 1. Make this tombstone big enough that statements can be written on it.

During the Session

1. At the beginning of class, present the tombstone prop. Explain that tombstones often represent our deep sadness and disappointment with life. Tombstones represent someone we've lost. At the same time, we've lost other things. We've watched hopes and dreams die in our lifes. Ask: *What has died in your life?* [See the first interactive of Day 1 on p. 41.] Ask learners to share their responses. Write some of the responses on the tombstone.

2. Ask a volunteer to read aloud John 11:21. After reading, review the events that have been discussed in the story of Lazarus in John 11. Then ask: *Has there been a time when you've asked the question: God, where were You in all this?* Expand this discussion to include the names of others who learners know that have questioned God's presence when disappointment struck. [See the second interactive of Day 1 on p. 41.] Follow up by asking learners to share how they responded to the interactive: *What contemporary issues make us wonder where God is?* (p. 42).

3. Ask: *How did you respond to the first interactive of Day 2 on page 43? Can faith and disappointment coexist?* Ask learners to explain their responses. Encourage learners to look at John 11. Ask learners to identify who in this story seems to reflect a sense of both disappointment and faith. Ask: *How honest are you with God regarding your feelings?* Use the last interactive of Day 2 (p. 45) to facilitate deeper discussion concerning honesty before God.

4. Ask: *What did Tony Evans mean when he talked about "resting in the faith of another." How did Martha model this notion?* Explain that Martha was encouraged by the fact that she knew who Jesus really was. Ask learners to share how they responded to the interactives on page 46 concerning the question, What do I *know* about Jesus and how does this affect me?

To the Leader:

Disappointment comes in many different colors. We've all been disappointed by people and circumstances. But do we let disappointment destroy our outlook? And more importantly, do we let disappointment destroy our faith? The brilliance of being a Christ follower is the fact that disappoint is not a crushing blow to God. He can meet us in our discouragement and give us faith!

Ask: *Based on Martha's claim in John 11:22, what claim can we make concerning struggles we face?* [See the last interactive of Day 3 on p. 47.]

5. Ask a volunteer to read aloud John 11:25-26. Ask learners to share how they understand these verses. Refer to the first interactive of Day 4 on page 48. Explain how Jesus was defining the resurrection as not simply some power He had. He personally is "the resurrection." The miracle of Lazarus's resurrection is reflective of a greater miracle, namely the resurrection of anyone who trusts Jesus. Ask: *Why is belief so essential for experiencing God's blessing?* [See the last interactive of Day 4 on p. 49.]

6. Read the following quotation from Day 5: "The real key to any kind of blessing from God is to verbally acknowledge who Jesus Christ really is—the Son of God, the all-powerful Second Person of the Trinity." Ask: *What does this quotation mean for us as we live out our faith?* Allow time for discussion. Keep the suggestions practical. Emphasize that knowing Jesus' identity is crucial. Ask learners to share their responses to Day 5's interactives on page 50. Ask: *What truth about Jesus has the most impact on you? How does it affect your life?* Allow time for discussion.

7. Close in prayer, asking God to increase our faith and help us know Him better through our disappointments and the devastating letdowns of life.

God, Do You Really Care ...When I Question You?

day One

Throwing Out the Red Flag

For a number of years now, the National Football League has employed a high-tech system called "instant replay," designed to help correct and possibly overrule the errors of game officials. According to the instant replay rule, the head coach of a team throws a red flag on the field when he thinks one of the officials missed a call—such as awarding a touchdown that shouldn't have been a touchdown or incorrectly ruling a receiver out of bounds on a pass play.

When the referee sees the red flag, he knows it's time to go to the coach to find out what the challenge is about. From there, he heads to the replay booth to review the call. Sometimes the call is reversed, but sometimes the referee rules that the play was too close to reverse—or that the covering official got it right the first time. In that case, the call stands and the team who challenged the ruling is charged with a timeout.

Some believers remind me of that football coach with the red flag. God makes a call in their lives, and they think He's gotten it wrong. They think He ought to review, reconsider, and even reverse the call. In short, they believe God has "blown it" and ought to make things right.

Can you think of a time when your initial reaction to God was thinking that He has "blown it"? If so, describe that situation in the margin.

I don't think there is a believer who has ever lived who hasn't at some point in his or her walk with Jesus questioned God and plainly asked Him, *Why me? Why now? Why this?* When we do that, what we're really asking

Him is whether He knows our situations, knows what He's doing in the midst of them, and really knows what's best for us.

Does God care when we question His wisdom, question His attentiveness, question His love?

I want to address that by looking at some interaction between Jesus and Martha as He was about to raise her brother Lazarus from the dead.

Jesus was about to perform the very miracle that the events recorded in John 11 had been leading up to, and as He approached Lazarus's stone-sealed tomb, He gave a very simple instruction: "Remove the stone."

We'd like to think that Martha would have just kept quiet and watched Jesus at work once the stone was removed. After all, just a few moments earlier she had acknowledged, "Even now I know that whatever You ask of God, God will give You" (v. 22).

Great words of confidence! But seconds later, when she heard Jesus' command to open up her brother's tomb, she threw the red flag. She wanted a review of that decision, pointing out what she knew to be a certainty, given the fact that Lazarus had been dead for so long: "Lord, by this time there will be a stench; for he has been dead four days" (v. 39).

What would you have done in Martha's situation? Would you have reacted in a similar or different fashion? _____ Why? _____

Martha was doing more than pointing out the obvious. Of course Jesus knew that a body lying in a grave for four full days would have the overpowering stink of death on it. In reality, what she was doing was questioning Jesus' instructions. What she was asking Him in reality was, "Why would You make such a request?" In her natural mind—one that still didn't fully comprehend what Jesus was about to do—opening that grave made no earthly sense.

How much of your life is driven by an earthly sense versus Jesus' kingdom sense? Mark your response below.

Earthly Sense   **Kingdom Sense**

The Struggle to Believe

To this day—perhaps now more than ever—people struggle when it comes to believing what God has said and doing what He has told them to do. Many of us, it seems, question Him, wanting to know "what's in it for us" if we take the step and obey Him. This is especially true when it comes to those things that seem unreasonable to us or "outside the box."

But John's account of the scene at Lazarus's grave shows us that it's the *tone* of the questioning that makes a difference to God.

Martha wasn't the only one at this scene questioning Jesus—nor the only one who wondered if He knew what He was doing. Earlier, I pointed out that some of those who had come from Jerusalem to Bethany to comfort Mary and Martha—including some, no doubt, who opposed Jesus—had a question of their own: "Could not this man, who opened the eyes of the blind man, have kept this man also from dying?" (v. 37).

There's a big difference in tone between the questioning of the unbelievers and that of Martha. On the one hand, there were already deep doubts—and cynicism so thick you could cut it with a knife. The Jews who had come to comfort the family weren't simply questioning Jesus, they were questioning His credentials as Messiah.

Who questions and challenges you because of your faith in Jesus? _____

How do you react to be being questioned?

_____

Martha, on the other hand, loved Jesus with all of her heart. And it was she who had earlier recognized Him as One who received from the Father's hand everything He asked for. While the unbelievers at the gravesite called Jesus "this man," Martha called Him "Lord."

Martha's perplexity was mixed with faith. Her questions and heartbreak were shot through with love. And Jesus was about to lead her into a deeper understanding of His nature and purpose.

To those who questioned Him and utterly dismissed His power over sickness and death, however, Jesus had nothing to say at all.

We all know how the Lazarus story ended—with the greatest miracle Martha or Mary or anyone else at the scene had ever seen. Before the miracle actually took place, however, Martha had no idea how the story would play out. Her mind, already locked up with grief and sorrow, simply could not process the turn of events. Jesus had not come when she and Mary called. But He had sent a message clearly stating that Lazarus's illness would not end in death. And then Lazarus died! And then Jesus arrived on the scene and told her that He was the resurrection and the life.

Nothing made sense.

Everything seemed in turmoil.

She still had no clue what Jesus had in mind for her and for Lazarus.

Even so, in spite of everything, in the face of all those questions-without-answers, she acknowledged Jesus as Lord.

Describe in the margin what it looks like for you to maintain faith in a "questions-without-answers" situation.

Then came that strange, disturbing command to remove the stone from the mouth of the tomb—and all she could think about was how bad the body was going to smell after four days.

Because we know in hindsight what Jesus was about to do, it might be easy for some of us to criticize Martha. After all, this was *Jesus* she was talking to, not just some man on the street. Of course she should have expected a miracle and of course she should have obeyed His command without questioning Him.

But I believe we need to cut Martha some slack here. First of all, if you've ever suffered deep grief, you'll know that it's hard even to think straight at these times. In truth, she was doing exactly what most of us would have done in that situation—responding to the natural facts as she knew them.

Jesus knew what was behind Martha's questions, but He was about to move her from the natural—from the facts of the world as she saw them—to a more spiritual level of thinking. He wanted her to catch a glimpse of the wonderful, miraculous plan He had for her life.

Knowing that we live in a natural world, how does it work in your life to have a spiritual level of thinking?

_____

What changes in our perspective when we employ a spiritual level of thinking? _____

God's Plan, Step by Step

We need to notice that Jesus had told Martha what He wanted her to do before He revealed what He would do. He didn't tell her, "Remove the stone and I will raise Lazarus from the dead." He simply said, "Remove the stone," a command that required a response from Martha.

But why didn't Jesus just tell Martha His whole plan when He gave the command for the stone to be moved? Because He was in the process of bringing her to a point of acting on what He already had told her, so that she could receive the blessing He had for her. This was a miracle-in-waiting, but it wasn't going to happen until the stone was moved.

Most of us want to know the details of what God is doing before we obey Him, don't we? We want just a little peek at His future plans for us before we sign on the dotted line. We want to know when we'll get that better job, when we'll find a mate, when things will change for us, when God will meet a particular need in our lives. That's why we tend to question God when He instructs us to do something that seems strange or even unreasonable.

As I said, God doesn't give us all the particulars of His plans for us. In fact, sometimes He doesn't tell us His plan at all. Sometimes He keeps some things secret from us until the time and situation are right.

And that might not be until eternity. Can we handle that?

In the Old Testament, it's described this way: "The secret things belong to the Lord our God, but the things revealed belong to us and to our sons forever, that we may observe all the words of this law" (Deut. 29:29).

In other words, while God sometimes reveals certain things to us, there are many other things He keeps secret and does not unveil for us until the time, the situation, and our hearts are right. It's important to understand that part of His character, and it's also important to know that oftentimes God won't reveal His *secret* will to us until we have been obedient to His *revealed* will.

God often reveals to us only what we need to know to take us to a particular point in His plan for us and only after we've taken that first step will He tell us what we need to know to get to the next step. In other words, when God has a plan to take us from point A to point C in our lives, He's not going to show us what point C is until we've obediently gone with Him to point B. If we aren't willing to go to point B—no matter how strange or confusing it may seem or no matter how it doesn't appear to fit into the plan of making it to point C—then God won't show us how He wants us to get to point C.

Sadly, many believers want to know the *whole* plan before they're willing to move the stone.

And why are we so often reluctant to move the stones God has told us to move? Simply because there are many times when His requests seem so strange to us.

How would you describe yourself when it comes to obeying God?
❑ **Reluctant**   ❑ **Responsive**

Why is it important for us to trust God faithfully even when we don't know the outcome?

In the margin, describe a situation when you felt like God's request seemed strange.

How can our faith be affected by situations where the end is uncertain? _____

day Four

Strange Commands

I don't want you to take this wrong, but in our human understanding God's logic can seem pretty weird sometimes. That's nothing new either, because the Bible is filled with examples of God commanding people to do some very strange things.

In the margin, make a list of biblical characters whom God called to do strange things.

Why, in Joshua 3, have the Jewish priests dip their feet in the flood-waters of the Jordan River so the people of Israel could cross? Why not just split the waters the way He did when Moses stretched out his rod over the Red Sea? Or better yet, why not supply everyone with boats?

Why, in Joshua 6, have the soldiers of Israel walk around the walls of Jericho quietly for six days, then have the priests blow their horns, when what they were looking for was a military victory? Why not just bless the troops with the supernatural ability to defeat the city militarily? Or easier still—why not just send fire and brimstone to take the city down and be done with it?

Why, in 2 Kings 5:10–14, have Naaman, the distinguished Syrian general, dip himself in the Jordan River seven times in order to heal him of leprosy? Why not just take it away miraculously by having someone lay hands on him?

Why, in John 9, give a blind man sight by smearing dirt and saliva in his eyes, then having him wash his face? Why not just heal him with a touch and a word and let him go on his way?

All of these incidents show us a God who sometimes does things in very strange and mysterious ways, ways that must have made the people involved wonder if God knew what He was doing. (Naaman himself at first refused to do as the prophet Elisha had said because it seemed so foolish, but when he did do what God said ... he was healed.) In each instance, God gave people very specific instructions that just didn't seem to fit in with what He was trying to accomplish.

But God has His reasons for doing things and commanding His people to do things that seem unreasonable or even a little crazy. In the examples cited above, God gave very specific—and seemingly bizarre—instructions and required exact obedience to the very letter. Why? Because He wanted to show His people they had nothing to lose and everything to gain by following His instructions, even those that might have seemed "off" to them.

We need to remember that our Heavenly Father is infinite in His wisdom and in His personal knowledge of each of His children. He knows precisely what it takes to test, deepen, and refine our faith. More often than not, our faith grows best against the backdrop of things we don't fully understand and not in the context of the things we do.

How has God put your faith to the test? _____

What "strange things" have you felt called to do?

_____

How has your "strange" situation affected your faith?

_____

Did I Not Say to You?

When Martha pointed out that there would be a terrible stench coming from Lazarus's tomb if the stone was removed, Jesus almost seemed impatient. Again, instead of telling her what He was going to do, He told her, "Did I not say to you that if you believe, you will see the glory of God?"

Let's focus on how Jesus began this reminder: "Did not I say to you." As Jesus gave Martha what sounded like a mild rebuke, He did so by bringing her attention back to what He already had said by reminding her that He had promised that Lazarus's illness wouldn't end in death and that Lazarus would rise again.

How do you typically respond to God's "mild rebuke"?

_____

How do you respond to the "mild rebuke" of a Christian brother of sister? _____

At this point in the story, Martha was in a very difficult place. She had taken her eyes off of Jesus' earlier promises and had focused instead on her present situation. In this moment she was focused on death, not on Jesus. And how had she come to this point? She had left God's word.

When we take our eyes off God and His word, we have nothing to look to but situations, speculations, and human reasoning.

In the margin describe how "situations, speculations, and human reasoning" have affected your capacity to make spiritually minded decisions.

BELIEVING BEFORE SEEING

God wants us to understand a simple but profound principle of faith: Believing comes before seeing. We must believe what He tells us before we can see what He intends to do.

So many of us have that backward, don't we? We live by the old saying "Seeing is believing" and want God to show us something before we believe Him and follow His specific directions.

That is exactly why Jesus asked Martha the "did I not tell you" question the way He did. He was essentially saying to her, "You don't need to tell Me that the body will smell bad. I'm well aware that your brother has been dead for four days. But that doesn't matter to Me because I'm about to do something to change all that. So if you're done questioning Me now, do as I asked you and move the stone."

Although we don't like to admit it, many of us question God simply because we don't really believe Him! And that's sad … because until we believe God, we can't expect to receive anything from Him.

What do you feel God has personally told you? Write your personal message from God below.

How much of your own faith experience is hampered by an unwillingness to believe God?
❑ It's greatly hampered.   ❑ It's seldom hampered.

Why do you feel this way? _____

Are you obeying His instructions or are you questioning what He said? _____

Read from your Bible what the apostle James wrote in James 1:6–8. According to James, what happens when our faith is weak? _____

Does this passage resonate with your own experience? ❑ Yes   ❑ No

How would you rate yourself as far as your commitment to do what God has told you to do?
❑ Highly Committed
❑ Somewhat Committed
❑ Not Committed

Why do you feel this way?

_____

_____

_____

We need to understand that our God doesn't waste words and He doesn't say something without having a reason for it or without expecting us to respond. When Jesus said, "Move the stone," He wasn't just speaking to hear Himself talk. There was a reason for those words, and it was to encourage Martha—and the others at the scene, including His disciples—toward a deeper faith and trust in Him, as well as a willingness to obey.

Let's face it, sometimes we're more interested in asking God questions than we are in simply hearing and obeying what He's already told us. Because of that, I believe, we miss His best for our lives.

When Jesus said, "Remove the stone," Martha had a decision to make, and it's the same one so many of us are faced with today. Will we focus on our questions about what God asks us to do, then allow those questions to become unbelief? Or will we commit ourselves to doing as God tells us to do, no matter what?

Martha would vote for the latter option.

Obeying a puzzling command led to the happiest day in her life.

Now complete the interactives in the margin.

Before the Session

Bring a local newspaper or two to class. You will use it for the opening exercise [see During the Session Step 1 below].

During the Session

1. As you begin your class, divide the local newspaper(s) into sections. Allow each learner to have a few pages. Ask learners to review their sections of the paper. Ask: *What were some of the things you read in your section of the paper?* After learners have shared, ask: *How many of the stories you read in the paper were likely the result of someone responding to the reality of God?* Explain that the newspaper is a great example of how we so often live our routines with little regard for God's presence in the world. Ask: *Why do you suppose it is easier not to allow God to be part of our daily routines?*

2. Ask a volunteer to read aloud John 11:38-39. Ask learners how they responded to the second interactive of Day 1 on page 54. Explain that Martha was thinking practically about Lazarus's body. Yet Jesus asked her to do something absurd—open the grave! Explain that sometimes God asks us to do things that don't make sense in earthly terms. Refer to the last interactive of Day 1 on page 54. Ask learners to share how they responded to this activity.

3. Say: *It is hard to think spiritually in a world that operates exclusively on an earthly level. People often question us because of our faith in Jesus.* Invite learners to share how they responded to the interactive on page 55. Ask: *How does their questioning affect your faith?* Allow time for discussion. Emphasize that we don't have to be afraid of the questions people pose. At the same time, we have to learn to live our faith in the midst of situations when there may not be a good answer. Ask learners to share how they responded to the remaining interactives of Day 2. Allow time for discussion of each item.

4. Say: *It's easy for us to look critically at the story in John 11. We get to see how the story turns out and then can look back on the events that led up to Lazarus's resurrection. Mary and Martha didn't have that luxury.*

To the Leader:

We live our lives within a world of calculated estimations. Yet we like certainty. Thus we rarely talk of making decisions based on the spiritual realities that seem so crucial in Jesus' Kingdom. This is not to say that we should criticize the practical way we live. Yet if we never venture into a world driven by faith in an unseen God, we will likely miss out on much. Help learners deal with the fact that we are called to live in such a way that we let the reality of Christ guide us into unimaginable and uncalculated places.

They simply saw God act in a step-by-step manner. Ask: *How would you describe yourself when it comes to obeying God?* [See the interactives on pp. 58-59.] Discuss the follow-up questions found in these interactives.

5. State: *Let's brainstorm. Who in the Bible comes to mind when you think about God making His people obey strange commands?* [See the first interactive of Day 4 on p. 59.] Ask: *Why do you think God tested people in the Bible with strange commands?* Allow time for responses. Emphasize that God operates the same way today! Refer to the last interactive of Day 4 on page 60 for further discussion.

6. Ask a volunteer to read aloud John 11:40. State: *Describe a time when you felt like God was rebuking you.* Direct learners to the first interactive of Day 5 on page 61.

7. Explain that it is hard to followthrough when God presents a strange request. Our human reasoning can take a toll on us. Remind learners of the newspaper articles they read at the beginning of class. Point out that we typically let reason rule the day. Refer to the interactives on the middle of page 61 and on the top of page 62.

8. Ask a volunteer to read aloud James 1:6-8. Have learners tell how they responded to the interactives on this passage in the middle of page 62. Ask: *How does this passage relate to our obedience and faith toward God?* Emphasize that God often wants us to trust Him—that's all!

9. Conclude this lesson by reviewing the last interactive of Day 5 found in the margin on page 62. Use this interactive to transition into a time of prayer with your group. Specifically focus on asking God to help us when we question Him, His plan, and His Word.

God, Do You Really Care ... When I Don't Believe?

day**O**ne

Learning to Believe Without Reservation

Most of us have the faith-thing down when it comes to the basics. We believe that Jesus is the one and only Son of God.

We believe He came to earth to die for our sins, so that we can live forever.

We even believe that God's Holy Spirit empowers us to live as He wants us to live and do the things He wants us as His children to do.

But there's a question some of us just aren't ready to tackle yet.

We have trouble believing God truly loves us and is working for our good when we are crushed by tragedy, pain, heartbreak, and loss. When our world collapses around us and we lose something we hold near and dear, we have a hard time believing God is really involved or that God really cares.

Does that matter to God? What do you think?

Does God notice and care when we don't believe?

I'd say He cares about that more than anything. Why? Because our whole relationship with Him is based on faith—our ability and willingness to believe Him and take Him at His word. And when we come to a place in our lives when our faith unravels into unbelief, He will do whatever it takes to restore our faith and bring us to a point of believing everything He has told us through His written Word, the Bible.

That is exactly what Jesus did with His dear friends Mary and Martha, women who believed in and loved Him but who somehow hadn't retained what He had already promised them.

Previously I pointed out how Jesus prepared the people at Lazarus's gravesite for a miracle when He made what seemed to be a very strange command: "Remove the stone." Martha responded to this command with what seemed to be a logical—and obvious—observation: "Lord, by this time there will be a stench; for he has been dead four days."

But now I want to focus on what Jesus replied to Martha in that moment—and what it meant to her ... and to us. When Martha made that comment about the stench, Jesus came back with a reply that sounded almost aggravated: "Did I not say to you that if you believe, you will see the glory of God?" (John 11:40).

If Jesus sounded a little impatient with Martha, it was because He wanted to drive home a point, and it's this: He had given her a promise, and it was a promise He fully intended to keep ... if she would only believe Him.

Once again, what promises has God given you?

_____

Has He fulfilled these, or are you still waiting?

_____

There is a very real connection between this statement and one Jesus made to His men before they left Perea to travel to Bethany. After telling a confused and frightened bunch of disciples that they would be going with Him to Bethany so they could awaken Lazarus from his sleep, Jesus finally got down to the meat and potatoes of His mission: "Lazarus is dead, and I am glad for your sakes that I was not there, *so that you may believe*" (vv. 14–15, emphasis mine).

Everything Jesus did and said in this account was for one purpose and that was that those who heard His words and saw His deeds would believe. He delayed coming to Lazarus's side so people would see the glory of God through Lazarus's illness ... and believe. He waited and was glad He did so simply so the disciples would see what was about to happen ... and believe. And He took the time to talk to Martha so she would hear His words and see His works ... and believe.

He does the very same thing for us today.

And belief is still a very, very important issue to Him.

Nothing is more important to God than having His children believe Him and His every word. God relates to each and every one of us on the basis of faith. So when we as believers come a point where life doesn't make sense, when we are going through a crisis that seems to have no meaning, when God seems completely absent in our situations, it may very well be that He is putting us in a place where we will learn to believe Him without reservation.

In the margin jot down your thoughts as to why you think Jesus prioritizes our learning to believe over and above His ability to immediately address our needs. Use John 11 to justify your response.

day *Two*

What It *Really* Means to Believe

In one sentence write down your definition of what it means to believe. _____

We've all heard sayings that go something like this: "God won't put you through more than you can bear."

There's a grain of truth to that. God can and will give us the strength to endure anything. But I think the premise of the saying is a little backward. Sometimes life's situations—the very ones God puts us in—can become literally unbearable.

But the Lord has a reason for that too. When God delays stepping into our life situations, when it seems He's put us in or allowed us to step into situations that we can't humanly bear, it's because He's up to something bigger, something of eternal value. And not only that, He is *glad* to do so because in the long run it stretches us and strengthens us and deepens our faith.

Describe in the margin a situation you or someone else has been through that could be described as unbearable. At the time of going through this situation, how would you (or the other person) have reacted if someone told you that God was simply trying to strengthen you?

In order to get a grip on this aspect of God's nature, we need to understand what it means to believe or to have faith. The writer of the Book of Hebrews defined faith as "the substance of things hoped for, the evidence of things not seen." He then continued, "For by it the elders obtained a good testimony. By faith we understand that the worlds were framed by the word of God, so that the things which are seen were not made of things which are visible" (Heb. 11:1–3, NKJV).

Faith, then, isn't a matter of what we can see, hear, smell, or touch. It's having the conviction or the assurance of something for which there is no empirical or physical support or proof. It's being absolutely convinced of some fact or truth, even though neither your physical senses nor human reasoning can grasp it, see it, smell it, or touch it.

The Bible very regularly makes the distinction between that which we know *by sight* and that which we know *by faith*. When you see something (or perceive it with any of your physical senses), you know it's there simply because the visual evidence tells you so. In other words, it's right before your eyes. But when you have faith in something God has told you or shown you, you can't always see it. Even so, you are convinced of its truth because you perceive it on a spiritual level.

That was exactly what Jesus was talking to Martha about when He said, "Did I not say to you, if you believe you will see the glory of God?" Jesus wanted Martha to understand with her heart and see with her spiritual eyes that He was real and that He was everything she had believed He was. He also wanted her to understand that *because* of who He was, she could believe and trust Him to keep His word to her.

We can believe everything God says, simply because it is not in His character to lie or to renege on a promise. He is the very embodiment of the word *trustworthy,* so we can count on Him completely.

Think about your own journey of faith. What experiences can you point out to verify the trustworthiness of God in your life? Write your response in the margin.

One thing God really loves is when we hold up His promises before Him and hold Him to His own word. That's because He loves showing His people that He is a God who is true to Himself and therefore true to His own words. To God this is not an "I dare you" challenge but a demonstration that we believe Him.

After working through today's reading, and specifically through the Scripture that was referenced, would you adjust your definition of what it means to believe? How? Respond in the margin.

day Three

Believing Means Taking Action

Many believers know what the Lord has *said* to them, but they don't seem to be able to make the connection between His words and what He's actually up to in their very own lives—especially when they're hurting or confused.

This is where Martha fell short.

Jesus gave a command to open up her brother's tomb, and all she could think about was how bad death would smell. Instead of making a connection between what Jesus already had said—both in His message from Perea and when He first spoke to her on His arrival in Bethany—and what He was about to do, she focused on the bare facts of the situation. *Lazarus was dead. Dead bodies decay. Rolling the stone away would be offensive.*

When Jesus prodded Martha by asking her, "Did I not say to you?" He was challenging her to pay closer attention to His word, to recall what He already had told her. That's the same challenge God gives us today, particularly in those times when we're hurting and life doesn't make much sense.

Jesus told Martha that if she believed, she would see "the glory of God." But what did that mean?

It meant that she was going to see *God being God.*

It meant that Jesus' absolute power over death would be put on display for her and everyone at the scene to see for themselves.

But there was a simple condition to this promise: She had to believe, and she had to demonstrate that belief by standing by Lazarus's grave as the stone was removed.

Think about the promises you believe God has given you in the past. How were you challenged by God to "act" in those situations? Write your response in the margin.

When we believe God, we take action based on what we know—that His word is truth. It's not based on what we can physically see, hear, and touch, and it's not based on what we can emotionally feel. There will be times in the life of every believer when feelings contradict what God is saying, when our emotions—as well as our rational minds—tell us that He's not really in control, that He's not really involved in our present situation, that He doesn't really care when we are sick, hurting, confused, or lacking the faith it takes to believe He will do what He's promised.

Have you ever felt that you missed out on seeing God move in your life simply because you didn't take action? _____ If so, describe briefly in the margin when and how this happened.

When Martha and Mary and the mourners who had come to comfort them stood before Lazarus's grave and heard Jesus tell them, "Remove the stone," they had been given a tangible way to demonstrate that they believed Him. I don't believe that was by accident, because I know that the same Jesus who can raise a man dead four days in the tomb could very easily have removed the stone without anyone's help. Jesus' command to have the people there remove the stone had nothing to do with His need for it to be moved. He could have had Lazarus walk right through it. But He was simply giving them an opportunity to put action behind what they believed—even though they had questions about the wisdom of that action.

We've all heard the old saying, "You talk the talk, but do you walk the walk?" We can apply that to how we demonstrate that we believe God because it's not just our words that demonstrate that we believe Him but also our actions. The apostle James pointed that out when he wrote, "What use is it, my brethren, if a man says he has faith, but he has no works?" (Jas. 2:14).

How well do you demonstrate that you believe God? Mark your response below.

❏ **Seldom**   ❏ **Often**   ❏ **All the time**

What is one way you can practically improve your demonstration of faith in your daily living?

_____

One Last Step Before a Miracle

With the stone out of the way, Jesus was ready to perform one of His best-known and most spectacular miracles. And as He made His final preparation to bring Lazarus out of the grave, He did what He so often did in key situations in His ministry.

He prayed.

John recorded the scene like this: "And Jesus lifted up His eyes and said, 'Father, I thank You that You have heard Me. And I know that You always hear Me, but because of the people who are standing by I said this, that they may believe that You sent Me'" (vv. 41–42, NJKV).

Jesus knew who He was.

He knew He was the Chosen One, the Son of God sent into the world to be our Savior. And He knew that He had the Father's ear and that He would receive anything He asked for. But we need to notice that Jesus didn't talk to the Father about what was about to happen until the people demonstrated they believed Him by removing the stone from the grave.

The Bible tells us that Jesus not only justifies us before God but also pleads with the Father on our behalf: "Who will bring a charge against God's elect? God is the one who justifies; who is the one who condemns? Christ Jesus is He who died, yes, rather who was raised, who is at the right hand of God, who also intercedes for us" (Rom. 8:33–34).

In the Bible, the word *intercession* means to "stand in the gap" on someone else's behalf. A good illustration of this is the work of a defense attorney—or, as some defendants might call him, "a mouthpiece"—who stands in the gap between a judge and jury on behalf of a client in a criminal court case. Because a defendant has an attorney pleading his case, he doesn't need to worry over whether his side of the story is being heard.

In the margin, make a list of the ways you believe Jesus intercedes on your behalf.

That is what Jesus does for all of us. We need to understand that without Him, the only answer we will ever receive from the Father is no, simply because we are guilty, lost in our sins, and without access to God. But because Jesus is at God's right hand taking our requests to the Father, we can know that God hears and responds and gives the Son what He asks for on our behalf.

When we are walking through difficult times, it's easy to spend a lot of time talking to others, debating with ourselves over what we want to do, and dwelling on our pain and confusion. But these are the last things we need to be doing during those times! The first thing we should do when we are hurting is take our problems to our intercessor, Jesus Christ. As we kneel before Him with hearts and minds of faith, He willingly steps into the gap between us and the Father.

That was the point of what Jesus was saying when He told His disciples, "If you abide in Me, and My words abide in you, ask whatever you wish, and it will be done for you" (John 15:7).

In the margin, describe ways that you "abide" with Christ. Pause right now and think about the issues you will face today and tomorrow. Ask Jesus to be your intercessor in the midst of your struggles.

Resurrections Multiplied

I can only imagine the initial reaction of those at the scene as they saw this body that had been dead four days walking out of the tomb and into the sunlight. At first, some of the people there had to be frightened— startled out of their wits—at seeing what had been a dead man walking. All had to have been in absolute awe at what they were seeing.

Open your Bible and read John 11:38–53.

But the event was more than sheer spectacle. Something else occurred that day—something with eternal significance. You might call it a chain reaction of life. A miracle raised Lazarus from the dead. And following on the heels of this, an even greater miracle swept through the crowd of previously unbelieving witnesses who saw a man emerge from death into the sunshine of life. "Therefore many of the Jews who came to Mary, and saw what He had done, believed in Him" (v. 45).

This is an example of one resurrection leading to many more, as many spiritually dead people on the scene were made alive that day. With their own eyes, they saw what Jesus had done and became convinced in their hearts that He was everything He had claimed to be, that He truly was the "resurrection and the life."

Of course there were some who still couldn't believe Jesus, even though He had responded to the faith of the few and raised a man from the dead. John reports that some of the people on the scene ran back to Jerusalem to tell the Pharisees what Jesus had done. John doesn't tell us the upshot of their reports. It's possible that some may have been moved to believe in

Jesus and wanted to tell their spiritual leaders about it. But it's also evident that many who went to the authorities were simply "ratting Jesus out."

The Pharisees, those learned men who had spent their lives studying the Scripture, had somehow missed the One who fulfilled everything the Old Testament had said about the coming Messiah. And when they heard the reports of this miracle, their response was to discuss how to stop Jesus before the entire nation of Israel believed in Him (vv. 46–53).

Why do you think the Pharisees, instead of being amazed, were frightened and threatened by Jesus?

_____

When it comes to bringing our hurts, grief, sickness, and confusion to God, we need to understand something. It is only when we demonstrate that we believe Him—and believe that He really cares when we are hurting—that we will see Him raise something from the dead in our lives. Yes, that kind of faith will almost certainly bring us opposition from those who don't believe. But it can also lead to life for those who hear us proclaim the name of Jesus Christ and watch as God does the miraculous for us.

How do you think people in today's world are frightened and threatened by Jesus?

_____

God cares when we don't believe, and He will take whatever steps are necessary in order to bring us to a point of believing Him and taking Him at His word. And when we come to that place, we'll have the privilege of seeing God's glory put on display in our own lives as well as in the lives of others around us.

And what will that look like?

It will be a picture of life out of death.

In the margin, suggest how you could express your testimony to others using the terminology of Jesus creating "a picture of life out of death" in your life.

Before the Session

Bring a microwave-safe dish and a pot you would use to cook on a stove. You will use these for the first During the Session Step 1 discussion item below.

During the Session

1. Place the microwave plate and the pot out for learners to see. Ask: *How has the microwave revolutionized the way we cook?* Help learners conclude that the microwave has given us the flexibility to speed up cooking. Cooking slowly on the stove is still doable; but if we need a quick meal, the microwave can give us what we need in minutes versus the longer stretch of time required for cooking on the stove. Explain that we have grown accustom to getting what we want with microwave speed. This is even the case when we think about how we expect God to respond to our needs and wants. We want a microwave response, not a slow cook on the stove.

2. Ask: *What did Martha and Mary want from Jesus—a microwave response or a slow cook response? Why do you suppose Jesus responded the way He did?* Ask learners to share their responses to the first interactives of Day 1 on page 66. Ask: *If you are still waiting for God to respond to the promise(s) He has given you, why do you suppose He has chosen a slower response?* Follow up by asking learners to share how they reacted to the last interactive of Day 1 on page 67.

3. Ask: *What do you think it means to believe?* [See the first Interactive of Day 2 on p. 67.] Ask a volunteer to read aloud Hebrews 11:1-3. Ask: *How does this passage affect your understanding of belief?* Emphasize that God always comes through for us. He is trustworthy. He certainly was for Mary and Martha. Ask learners to share how they responded to the interactives on the top of page 69.

4. Review John 11:38-44. Ask: *How did Jesus ask people to "act" in this situation?* Invite learners to share how they responded to the first interactive of Day 3 on page 70. Explain that acting is extremely important if we are to grasp the power of faith in our lives. Ask learners to share their

responses to the second and third interactives of Day 3 on pages 70-71. Allow time for discussion. Explain that our demonstration of faith is extremely important.

5. Ask a volunteer to read aloud John 11:41-42. Ask: *Why do you suppose Jesus prayed this way?* Explain that one of the great realities regarding Jesus is the fact that He intercedes for us. Ask learners to share their responses to the interactive activity on page 72. Ask: *How do we experience Jesus' intercession for us?* Explain that His intercession is felt as we abide in His presence. Read aloud John 15:7. Follow-up by asking learners to share their responses on the last interactive exercise in Day 4 on page 73. Allow time for discussion. You may wish to lead learners in a prayer related the issues they named.

6. Ask learners to close their eyes and listen as you read aloud John 11:38-53. Ask: *As you heard these verses, what did you visualize concerning how Lazarus came out of the tomb? What do you imagine it looked like?* Ask learners to review their responses to the first two interactives on page 74. Say: *Jesus is controversial, even when we consider all the amazing things He has done! Nevertheless, Jesus continues creating life in the midst of death!*

7. Conclude this lesson by letting learners respond to the final interactive of Day 5. Lead learners in a prayer asking God to help us to believe even when we experience feelings and thoughts of unbelief and to help us reflect before our friends, coworkers, and acquaintances the new life Jesus has given us.

God, Do You Really Care ...When I'm Trapped?

"Unbind Him and Let Him Go!"

Have you ever been literally trapped? Maybe stuck in an elevator or locked into a room or someplace you couldn't get out of? If so, you know it can be at the very least frustrating ... and sometimes downright frightening.

Turn in your Bible and read John 11:43–44. Describe a time when you felt trapped.

_____

From the eleventh chapter of John we've been learning about Lazarus, the object of one of our Lord's most incredible miracles. But even after Jesus raised Lazarus from the dead, the former corpse was *still* literally trapped. He may have been out of the tomb, but he still wasn't completely free.

Let me explain.

After the people in Bethany had done what it took to demonstrate that they believed Jesus—removed the stone from the grave—and after Jesus prayed, He finally did what He had come to do in the first place.

"Lazarus, come forth," Jesus called out, and that is exactly what happened. This man, whose dead body had been rotting in that dark cave for four full days, shocked everyone on the scene when he got up and walked to the mouth of the tomb. Lazarus truly was alive again. The body that four days earlier had ceased to function now resumed operating as though he had never even been sick, let alone dead.

But Jesus wasn't finished with Lazarus yet.

John tells us there was still a problem when it came to Lazarus continuing a normal life: "The man who had died came forth, bound hand and foot in wrappings, and his face was wrapped around with a cloth" (v. 44).

You see, Lazarus was literally in bondage, tied up head to toe in the burial wrappings the Jewish people traditionally put around the bodies of those who had died. Lazarus must have looked like the mummy we've all seen in those old Boris Karloff pictures, except that the mummy in those movies could move his arms and hands and legs freely—and see well enough to chase down the archeologists who had disturbed his sleep!

Even though Lazarus was alive again, in a very real sense death was still holding him down. Yes, he was up and he was out. But he still wasn't free. He could barely move his arms and legs, and he couldn't see a thing. But Jesus was about to finish what He had started. He had given Lazarus new life, but now He would give him freedom as well.

"Unbind him and let him go!"

Moments before, the people at the gravesite had demonstrated a measure of faith by obediently removing the stone that had sealed Lazarus's tomb. When they again obeyed, Lazarus was free from the trappings of death—free to be physically alive and—more than that—to actually live.

In a very real sense, that is what Jesus does for each and every one of us today. Sadly, however, too many of us who have received His gift of eternal life are living our lives here on earth as though we don't know that Jesus has freed us. We aren't talking right, walking right, or moving right, simply because the trappings of death still have us in their grip.

In other words, we're still walking around in our grave clothes.

What do you think it means to say that you are still walking in "grave clothes"?

_____

_____

_____

Freed for a Purpose

Jesus once told a group of Pharisees who were questioning Him, "The thief comes only to steal and kill and destroy; I came that they may have life, and have it abundantly" (John 10:10). To me, this implies that there is more to knowing Jesus Christ as our Lord and Savior than just waiting around to die so we can go to heaven. It tells me that Jesus wants to give us a life of freedom, a life that reflects what He's done for us in the eternal sense.

It's a life Jesus wants us to live *here and now.*

But why, if Jesus came to give us abundant life and true freedom, are so many believers more like "dead men walking" than the living, breathing reflections of the life Jesus came to bring? Why are they still tied up and trapped in their problems, in their addictions, in their strongholds? Why are they still bound up in the clothing of death when Jesus has given them life eternal? I believe it's because there are many of us who don't even realize just how free we really are.

But that can change. Maybe even today.

Write your definition of spiritual freedom in the margin.

THE EXPERIENCE OF FREEDOM

On June 19, those of us who live in the great state of Texas celebrate a holiday we call "Juneteenth," which commemorates the final granting of freedom to slaves in this state on that date in 1865.

President Abraham Lincoln's Emancipation Proclamation went into effect on January 1, 1863, which meant that all slaves in the rebel states were legally free. After the end of the Civil War and the defeat of the South, slavery should have ended in all states. But that didn't happen in Texas until June 19, 1865, when Union General Gordon Granger rode into Galveston and read General Order #3, which began, "The people of Texas are informed that, in accordance with a proclamation from the Executive of the United States, all slaves are free."

At that point, former slaves all over Texas started packing their bags and heading out for other states, hoping to make better lives for themselves as free men and women.

As far as federal law was concerned, the slaves in Texas had been legally freed on January 1, 1863. But as far as actually *experiencing* that freedom, it took another two-and one-half years.

Why did it take so long? Because during the Civil War, the Union armies never successfully invaded Texas, and the practice of slavery continued to flourish. In fact, many slave owners from other states came to Texas and brought their slaves with them to wait out the war, hoping that the Confederacy would win. Wealthy, powerful, and influential, Texas slaveholders were able to squelch and suppress the news of the Emancipation.

This piece of Texas history demonstrates something we as Christians need to understand. Freedom doesn't mean anything unless we know we are free and can actually enjoy and live in that freedom.

JESUS' MISSION OF FREEDOM

Early in His ministry, Jesus traveled to His hometown of Nazareth, where He attended the local synagogue. When the leaders gave Him the scroll of the prophet Isaiah—a prophecy written hundreds of years back in Israel's history—he read these words to those who assembled that day: "The Spirit of the Lord is on me, because he has anointed me to preach good news to the poor. *He has sent me to proclaim freedom for the prisoners* and recovery of sight for the blind, *to release the oppressed,* to proclaim the year of the Lord's favor" (Luke 4:18–19, NIV, emphasis mine).

The simple reading of that passage didn't raise any eyebrows; His audience had heard those words many times before. But moments later Jesus rocked them back on their heels with something they had never heard before—*"Today this Scripture has been fulfilled in your hearing"* (Luke 4:21, emphasis mine).

In other words, Jesus was telling the crowd, "You've been waiting for your Messiah and looking forward to the freedom He is coming to bring you. Well, you're looking at Him right now. I am that Messiah."

What do you think spiritual freedom should look like?

Does your life reflect such spiritual freedom? Mark your response. ❏ **Seldom** ❏ **Never** ❏ **Often**

Why do you feel this way about the impact of spiritual freedom in your life?

The Look of Freedom In Christ

The apostle Paul spoke a great deal about our freedom in Christ.

Read the following verses in your Bible that tell us what Christ has freed us from and then match each item on the left to its reference on the right by drawing a line to connect them.

The bondage of sin	1 Cor. 15:56–57
Spiritual death	Gal. 2:4–5
Bondage to the law	Rom. 6:17–18
The guilt and condemnation of sin	Col. 1:21–22
The power of sin and death	Rom. 6:23
Human regulations	Rom. 8:1
The enemy's false accusations	Rom. 7:4–6

When we first come to Jesus Christ in faith, we are given eternal life and our destiny in heaven with Him is sealed. Eternal life—life at a higher level—begins the moment you say yes to Christ. But some of us are still walking around in grave clothes, dragging around the trappings of death wherever we go. That is literally what Lazarus did when he first came out of the grave, and it is spiritually what so many of us do even after we've been saved.

But there is something we need to catch when it comes to receiving new life and then walking in that life. When Jesus raised Lazarus from the dead, He still had more work to do—the relatively minor task of removing the trappings of death, trashing the old shroud. It would only be after these trappings were removed that Lazarus would be completely free to resume his life as a friend and follower of Jesus.

Before someone accepts Jesus Christ as Savior, he or she is spiritually dead in trespasses and sin and well on the way to eternal separation from God. But upon conversion, something miraculous happens: That person is made *spiritually alive,* just as Lazarus was made *physically alive* the moment Jesus called him out of the tomb.

"Living a life of faith means knowing that Jesus has given us freedom from the wardrobe of the tomb."
—Tony Evans

What I want you to think about is this: If Jesus could raise what was absolutely dead and stinking to life, how much more is He able to remove the trappings of death so that the one who was once dead can start living—really living—the life He has for us!

Living a life of faith means knowing that Jesus has given us freedom from the wardrobe of the tomb. And never forget that this mighty release has an impact both in eternity and in the right-here-and-now. He has released us from the chains of sin and death and given us eternal life in heaven, and He has set us free from everything that keeps us from living a life that pleases God.

Knowing we are free in Christ motivates and empowers us to be the kind of Christ-followers who make a difference in the world around us, the kind who give freely out of the freedom we have received.

Think about the definition of "spiritual freedom" that you wrote under Day 2. Based on today's study, how would you revise your definition?

_____

_____

Free to Free One Another

Lazarus's situation when he first stepped out of the dark mouth of that tomb was that he was "bound hand and foot with wrappings." That must have meant he was barely able to make his way out of that cave and into the sunlight, let alone walk, talk, and see freely. Obviously, Lazarus was bound so tightly and so head-to-toe that he needed to be set free from his "burial suit."

"Unwrap him and let him go" contains a principle, and it is this: God wants to use those of us He already has freed to help free others. The Gospel of Matthew tells us that after the disciples had spent time with Jesus listening to His teaching and observing His miracles, He sent them out on their first "missionary journey" with these marching orders: "Heal the sick, raise the dead, cleanse the lepers, cast out demons. Freely you received, freely give" (Matt. 10:8).

Earlier in this lesson I listed some of the things the apostle Paul told us Jesus frees us *from*. But Paul also told us throughout his letters that we are also freed *for* certain actions and privileges. Because we know Jesus Christ as our Lord and Savior, there are things we get to do freely in His name.

**Read the following verses in your Bible that tell us
what we may freely do in Christ's name and then
match each item on the left to its reference on the
right by drawing a line to connect them.**

Serve Christ	Eph. 3:12
Serve others in the name of Christ	1 Cor. 7:22
Seek only God's best for others	1 Cor. 9:19
Serve one another in love	1 Cor. 10:23–24
Approach our Heavenly Father confidently	Gal. 5:13

Did you notice? Many of the things the Bible says we are free to do involve "doing" for others in the name of Jesus. When Jesus said, "Freely you have received, freely give" (Matt. 10:8), it was a command. He never intended for us to hoard our blessings or take our freedom for granted.

If God has made you spiritually alive through your faith in Jesus Christ, then "unwrapped" you from the trappings of death, you'll be ready to help out when someone else needs to be freed. And you won't have to look very far ... open your eyes and you will see people staggering about in grave clothes all around you.

How do you help free people from the trappings of death? It begins as you express your willingness to God and allow the Holy Spirit to show you what to do and to bring needy people across your path. For example, if Jesus has delivered you from a specific sin, habit, or addiction, you may have the opportunity to help free someone else who is still tied up in the same thing. If He has freed you to enjoy a strong and happy marriage, then you may have a chance to help out someone else whose marriage is struggling.

Indicate in the margin specific ways the "freedom of Christ" has opened doors for you to serve others.

But how do you find those opportunities to help lead others into the full freedom Jesus came to bring them? It starts by taking the time to build intimacy with Him, something anyone who has been freed from death and its entanglements will be motivated to do.

From the Tomb to the Table

John records an interesting and telling scene a short time after Jesus raised Lazarus from the dead. It's a clear demonstration of what happens when Jesus gives us life and then releases us from our cemetery outfits.

According to John 12:1–2, what was that event?

In the Bible, when we read the word *reclining*, it usually refers to spending time breaking bread with someone, to fellowshiping and building intimacy with that person.

We should pay special attention to how Lazarus responded to the miracle Jesus had done for him. Jesus had just given Lazarus life and also made sure that he was freed from the trappings of death. As a result, Lazarus was pursuing a deeper relationship with the Lord. Already a good friend of Jesus, he now wanted that friendship to be more close and intimate than ever.

What would you think of this man Lazarus if he had shrugged away his resurrection and said it wasn't a big deal? What would you think if he acted as though he had never been freed from death and its trappings? What if he took a casual, nonchalant attitude toward Jesus, and pushed the friendship to one side? We would say, "What an ungrateful lout! What's wrong with that man?"

But isn't that how we respond to our Lord when we take our eternal salvation for granted, accept our promised freedom with a yawn, and neglect our relationship with Him? How can we be "casual" with the One who has called us out of darkness and death and released us from its putrid wrappings?

When Jesus raises you from the dead, and in the spiritual sense then "unwraps" you from the trappings of death, your heart should leap toward intimacy with Him. When you think of what He has done for you, how could you not want to be with Him, and enjoy His friendship? As with Lazarus, you will want to "recline with Him at the table" always and learn more about Him and His heart's desire for you.

FREEDOM FROM FEAR

According to John 12:9–11, how did the religious leaders respond to the news of Lazarus's resurrection?

_____

What did they attempt to do?_____

Why did they want to do this? _____

John tells us that there was a death threat on the resurrected man's head. The news of Lazarus's resurrection made its way around the Jerusalem area very quickly, and some of the people who had heard about it were none too pleased. These were the chief priests and Jewish religious leaders who now not only wanted Jesus put to death, they wanted to kill Lazarus too! Why would they do such a thing? Because what Jesus had done for Lazarus had led many of the Jews to believe in Him. And that just couldn't be tolerated.

This is the only time in history that I know of where a man who had already died was threatened with death—and it happened for one reason: Lazarus's new life was bringing attention to the Lord Jesus Christ!

I can't help but think that the religious establishment's response didn't bother or frighten Lazarus all that much. After all, *he already had been dead!* He knew there was nothing they could do to him that Jesus couldn't handle. And maybe he also knew something that few men in history could ever know … that death wasn't such a bad prospect after all.

Lazarus's "new" life principle was that nothing—not even threats to his life—was going to keep him from associating freely and openly with the One who not only gave him new life but who also freed him from the trappings of death.

The question each of us who believes in Jesus Christ must ask is this: *Who is coming to Jesus because of me?* Each of us who knows Jesus as our Lord and Savior has been called and made alive in Him. And we've also been "unwrapped" or liberated from the accessories of death, freeing us from the power of sin and death to be a testimony for Him.

Yes, God cares when we are trapped. He cares so much that He sent His Son to free us from the power of darkness, both here on earth and in the eternity to come. And when Jesus makes us "free indeed," we can respond in no other way than to draw nearer to Him, so near that people around us see our identification with Him. When that happens, others will be drawn to Jesus and to the freedom He offers in such wonderful abundance.

How would you answer the question, Who is coming to Jesus because of me?

Before the Session

Bring a blindfold to class. You will use this for an illustration in During the Session Step 1 below.

During the Session

1. Ask a volunteer to read aloud John 11:43-44. Ask learners to share how they responded to the first interactive of Day 1 on page 77. Ask for a volunteer who will allow you to put a blindfold on him or her. After placing the blindfold on this person, ask: *Physically, you still have the capability to see, correct? With the blindfold you can't see, right?* Have the volunteer take off the blindfold. Say: *The blindfold symbolizes a spiritual problem we often experience. In the case of the blindfold, the person with his or her eyes covered has the ability to see but he or she can't because the blindfold hampers his or her sight. In the same way, spiritually speaking, many of us have the ability to really live, but, like being blindfolded, our ability is hampered. This was the image Lazarus presented—alive but wrapped up in grave clothes.* Ask learners to share how they responded to the interactive on the bottom of page 78.

2. Ask: *How would you define spiritual freedom?* Explain that spiritual freedom is something profound and amazing. Ask a volunteer to read aloud Luke 4:18-19. Ask: *What do these verses say to us about freedom?* Lift up the blindfold and explain that so many of us have failed to grasp the fact that Jesus calls us to live with a sense of freedom but we still choose to put on the blindfold. Ask: *Why do you suppose we don't want to experience this freedom?* Review the interactives at the end of Day 2 on pages 80-81.

3. Look at the first interactive of Day 3 on page 81. Have learners read each of the Scripture references listed. Ask: *Of the Scripture references listed, which ones mean the most to you? Why?* Allow time for responses. Explain that we as human beings all need to be rescued from something. Jesus is the only One to offer true freedom. Ask learners to share how they responded to the final interactive of Day 3 on page 82. Specifically ask learners to share how they are revising their understanding of spiritual freedom.

To the Leader:

Sometimes the hardest realities of life are the ones we simply can't escape. Many of us feel trapped by our circumstances. We need to know that God can meet us in the midst of our helplessness. Lazarus was described as alive, but he was still bound in his grave clothes. Many of us are alive, but we are still wrapped up in binding "grave clothes." Jesus wants us to experience more than simply living and breathing. He wants us to genuinely live life in its fullest!

NOTES

4. Once again, have learners look up the verses listed in the first interactive of Day 4 on page 83. Ask: *Of the Scripture references listed, which ones mean the most to you? Why?*

5. Explain that there is great power in understanding that we are called to actively serve and help others. Our faith is not a selfish endeavor. Instead, it involves our willingness to look beyond ourselves. Discuss how learners responded to the final interactive of Day 4 on page 84.

6. Ask a volunteer to read aloud John 12:1-11. Ask: *What happened after Lazarus's resurrection?* Ask learners to share how they responded to the interactives on pages 84 and 85. Say: *It causes a stir when Jesus affects us. This was the case for Lazarus. His miracle-life caused people to be both amazed and angry. How about you? Jesus saved you! You have been transformed into a miracle-life. How does your miracle-life impact the world around you? How do people react to your changed life?* Allow time for responses to and discussions of each of these questions.

7. Ask learners to share their reactions to the final interactive of Day 5 on page 86—"Who is coming to Jesus because of me?"

8. Close your time in prayer, asking God to free learners from that which traps them and to liberate them so they can personally enjoy and then tell others about the new life Jesus has given them.

Oh, Yes, He Cares!

day One

A Letter of Encouragement

Turn in your Bible to Hebrews 4:14-16 and meditate on the words found there.

If ever a group of people needed the message "God cares," it was the first-century believers in the fledgling church in Jerusalem.

Christians in that time and place faced fierce opposition from both the Jewish religious establishment and the Roman government. Within decades following the establishment of the church, Rome had adopted an official policy of persecution of Christians. Because of that, these believers faced rejection from their friends, family, and fellow country-men; the confiscation of their land and other personal property; and even imprisonment and death.

All because they believed in and served Jesus Christ!

Many of these believers became so deeply discouraged that they were close to throwing in the towel. They, like Mary and Martha when Jesus first arrived on the outskirts of Bethany, had to be wondering where Jesus was or whether He really cared that they were suffering.

Nothing will shake a believer's faith like believing the Devil's lie that Jesus doesn't really care when His people suffer—or that if He does care, there's really nothing He can do about it. But in the midst of all this perse-cution, suffering, and discouragement a letter of encouragement arrived— a letter we've come to know as the New Testament Book of Hebrews.

The writer, unknown to us today, assured these stressed, suffering people that Jesus cared very much about what they were enduring and that He was there for them to give them what they needed to hold on.

One of the most encouraging passages in the entire Bible is found in Hebrews 4. In it the writer assures believers that Jesus not only cares when we're facing tough times but that He takes action on our behalf in the very midst of them.

Read Hebrews 4:14–16 in your Bible. Who is our great high priest? _____

Why can He sympathize with our weaknesses?

_____

How should this affect us? _____

day *Two*

Our *Great* and *Heavenly* High Priest

Most Christians today really can't grasp the role of the first-century high priest. And yet this was an understanding deeply woven into the culture and religious lives of devout first-century Jews in the days of the early church.

Jewish people knew the high priest as the mediator or representative between the ordinary, average person and a holy God. They knew the high priest as the one responsible for presenting sacrifices to God on the annual Day of Atonement so their sins could be covered for the whole year.

The main theme of the Book of Hebrews is the high priesthood of our Lord Jesus Christ. The writer of this letter refers to Him as "a merciful and faithful high priest in service to God … that he might make atonement for the sins of the people" (2:17, NIV) and as "the apostle and high priest whom we confess" (3:1, NIV).

Hebrews identifies Jesus as the New Covenant replacement for the human high priesthood, which God had put in place temporarily and as a forerunner to the ultimate once-and-for-all sacrifice of Jesus Christ, the eternal Son of God, on the cross. It showed early Jewish Christians that

Jesus fulfilled every requirement God had for the forgiveness of sins and the redemption of humankind.

Obviously, the office of high priest was incredibly important to the Jews. The high priest wasn't elected by the people but was chosen by God Himself, and the responsibilities of the office were awesome. But the writer of Hebrews goes to great lengths to explain the superiority of Jesus over a sacrificial system that employed a human high priest. He refers to Jesus as a "*great* high priest," identifies Him by His human name—Jesus Christ—then by His eternal title—the Son of God.

A HEAVENLY HIGH PRIEST

Hebrews 4:14 not only identifies Jesus as the Son of God but it also tells us something else we might find easy to overlook: Jesus the great High Priest "passed through the heavens."

But what does it mean to us that Jesus passed through the heavens?

As I pointed out earlier, in Old Testament times the Jewish high priest was solely responsible for performing the sacrifices during the annual Day of Atonement. It was on this day that the high priest entered into the tabernacle by passing through the outer court, walking through the inner court, then into the very presence of God. There in the holy of holies, he sprinkled blood on the mercyseat—the act that made it possible for God to forgive the sins of His people for another year.

When the writer of Hebrews spoke of the "great high priest who has passed through the heavens," he was using a word picture Jewish readers would have immediately understood. What it declared was Jesus' presence in all three parts of the temple—the outer court, the inner court, and the presence of God Himself in the holiest of holies.

Jesus our High Priest went back into the very presence of God the Father, where He represents us before Him. And while the best an earthly high priest could do was to represent the people before God once a year, on the Day of Atonement, our High Priest sits at the right hand of God, pleading our case 24/7!

So what is the writer of Hebrews telling us is so special about our High Priest? Simply that He gives us something all of us need—access to God Himself.

As you contemplate your faith, what does it mean to say that you have "access to God"? _____

How does this affect the way your live your life?

_____

Access to the Father

There's a story (one I am told is true, or at least based in fact) of a soldier sitting on a park bench in Washington D.C. at some point during the Civil War. The man obviously was distraught, and when a small boy happened by the bench he noticed that this soldier was weeping.

"What's wrong, sir?" the lad asked, and the soldier told him that he desperately needed to see President Abraham Lincoln but had been denied access to the president's office. "Take my hand and follow me," the little boy offered, and then he led the soldier up to gate of the president's mansion, past the guards, and into the mansion itself. The boy led the soldier right into the office of Abraham Lincoln himself!

"Father," the boy said, "this soldier needs to talk to you."

How does this illustration relate to the relationship between God and us? Use Hebrews 4:14-16 to help explain your response in the margin.

There's something very empowering about knowing the son of a person of power, isn't there? And that is our position and unspeakable privilege as those who know Jesus Christ as Lord and Savior.

Because we know the One who sits at the right hand of the Father, who has His ear, and who receives everything He asks of the Father, we have access to the Father Himself.

Having that kind of amazing, incomprehensible right of entry, the writer tells us, is the very reason we should remain confident and steadfast in our faith—even in the face of heartbreak, pain, and trials. "Therefore, since we have a great high priest who has passed through the heavens, Jesus the Son of God, *let us hold fast our confession*" (v. 14).

In other words, the writer of Hebrews was telling those first-century Jewish believers, *Don't quit! Don't turn away from your faith in Jesus Christ simply because you are persecuted and suffering. Hold on to your confidence, because you have been granted entry into the presence of the very Creator of the universe, because you know His Son.*

What pressures you to "quit" your faith in Jesus?

_____

What helps you remain strong in your faith?

_____

They must have wondered the same thing many believers today still wonder when they endure difficult or painful times: Where is Jesus *right now?*

Maybe you've asked that question just lately. Perhaps even today.

You want and need to know where God is when you are sick, when you are grieving, when you are suffering, and when you don't really know for sure that He even cares about your personal situation.

There's an answer to those kinds of questions. It's simple, it's wonderful, and it's right in the very portion of Scripture we've been looking at.

day *Four*

Perfect Sympathy and Confident Weakness

We know by faith that God is in His heaven and that He demonstrates a measure of control over everything that happens down here on earth.

But as we wrestle with our problems day by day, we begin to think of God as "far away" and wonder if He really cares about our personal lives.

The writer of Hebrews encourages us to "hold fast to our confession," or, as another version of the Bible puts it, "never stop trusting him" (4:14, NLT). But this passage gives us further encouragement, telling us, "We do not have a high priest who cannot sympathize with our weaknesses, but One who has been tempted in all things as we are, yet without sin" (v. 15).

It's important to focus closely on the wording of this verse because it tells us something very, very important that we need to know about our relationship with Jesus. *He understands what we're going through because He's been there Himself.*

The writer of Hebrews uses the word *sympathize,* which carries with it the idea of actually suffering with someone who hurts, even to the point of feeling what they feel. It's one thing to listen to someone pour out his or her hurts, understand how that person feels, and even grieve for that person. But it's a whole other level of caring when we personally enter into that person's pain and grieve *with* him or her.

What best qualifies someone to actually sympathize with someone in need and pain? Simply having experienced the same things that person has experienced. As the old saying goes, "You have to walk a mile in their shoes."

Think about some of the most difficult trials you have been through. How can Jesus sympathize with what you've been through? Write your thoughts in the margin.

That, friends, is exactly what Jesus did when He left His Father in heaven, came to earth, and spent 33 years living among humans in human form.

Jesus is infinitely superior to any earthly high priest because He's not limited to mere human understanding when it comes to our pain and weakness. While an earthly priest could give you words of comfort and some understanding, Jesus has given Himself to actually feeling anything and everything we feel.

But there is more. Jesus is like those of us who live in a fallen, sinful world in that it was sin that ultimately did Him in. Jesus personally experienced the penalty for sin, which is death. The difference between Him and us in that respect, however, is that it wasn't *His* sin—because He was without sin—but *our* sin that led to His death on the Cross.

So … if Jesus was without sin, how can He understand me, a sinful creature, and my weaknesses?

The apostle Paul wrote, "He made Him who knew no sin to be sin on our behalf, so that we might become the righteousness of God in Him" (2 Cor. 5:21). This tells us that while Jesus lived a life of sinless perfection, He still knew how it felt to be separated from His Father because of sin.

When we take our pain, confusion, and weaknesses to Jesus, we aren't taking them to someone who just hears and understands (as important as that is) but to someone who actually *feels* our pain with and for us, someone who fully understands and sympathizes with our every human weakness.

The writer of Hebrews tells us that Jesus is our High Priest who sympathizes with our weaknesses and helps us when we do one thing—draw near to the throne of grace.

How have you traditionally thought God feels about your sin? Circle all that apply.
(a) offended   (b) angry   (c) disappointed
(d) fed-up   (e) compassionate   (f) Other: _____

How does your responses measure up to the Scriptures investigated in this discussion?

_____

CONFIDENT WEAKNESS

All of us have weaknesses.

Notice that in the passage we've been looking at it doesn't say that Jesus sympathizes with us *if* we have weakness. It just assumes that we all have them. And we have a High Priest who cares about them.

The good news for us, however, appears one verse later: "Therefore let us draw near *with confidence* to the throne of grace, so that we may receive mercy and find grace to help in time of need" (v. 16).

This verse describes what I call approaching God from a position of "confident weakness." First, we have in Jesus a High Priest who sympathizes with our weaknesses. Second, we have been invited to approach Him, acknowledging our need. But third, and perhaps most importantly, it means we approach Him *with confidence,* knowing that He wants more than anything to give us sympathy, grace, mercy, and help in our time of need.

Is there a condition to receiving this help from God?

Yes, there is.

And it's found in understanding what the throne of grace really is, and who occupies it.

How do you typically approach God?
❑ **Timidly**   ❑ **With confidence**

Does your "typical approach" agree with what is revealed in Hebrews 4:16? _____ Why or why not?

Who's On the Throne?

When we approach our Heavenly Father, we need to remember that we are approaching the One who sits on the throne, the One who is in charge, and the One who decides everything that happens in our lives. This means that while Jesus sympathizes with us in our weaknesses, it is the Father who chooses how to help us in those weaknesses.

When a parent sees his child's pain and doesn't intervene in the situation the way the child wants, it doesn't mean that the parent doesn't sympathize. It also doesn't mean the parent doesn't have the child's very best in mind.

The very same thing is true with our Heavenly Father.

There isn't a believer around who hasn't during a time of weakness pleaded with God to step into a situation and intervene in a specific way-only to find that He wouldn't do it. But that didn't mean that God didn't care, only that He was acting both for His own glory and for the best for His child.

Right about now, you're probably asking, "What good is God's sympathy if He's not doing for me what I hope for and desire?" That's an excellent question, but the truth is that when we approach God's throne, we will always get something, even if it's not what we think we need.

It's called *grace*.

But what exactly is *grace*? It's simply God doing for us what we can't do for ourselves. It's God supplying us with what we need—even if it's not what we *want* or *think* we need—until He steps in and changes our situation.

Unfortunately, a lot of us want to dictate to the throne of God during our times of want. Too many have been influenced by the "name it and claim it" preachers out there who teach that God is somehow obliged to do for us what we say and how we say to do it, simply because we're one of the King's kids.

God will always allow us as His children to approach His throne of grace with confidence, and He will always sympathize with us, but He will never let us dictate how He's going to handle the situations we bring before Him. God will always be God, and He will never share His sovereignty with anyone.

> "God will always allow us as His children to approach His throne of grace with confidence, and He will always sympathize with us, but He will never let us dictate how He's going to handle the situations we bring before Him."
> —Tony Evans

Where in your life right now do you need to experience a touch of God's grace? _____

WHEN WILL HE ACT?

Hebrews 4:15–16 contains one of the greatest promises in the Bible, which is that God will not only sympathize with us in our weaknesses but that He also will freely dispense the mercy, grace, and help we need to endure.

But still you may be asking, "When is God going to step in and resolve my situation?"

Well, I can't tell you that. As a minister of the gospel of Jesus Christ, I am obligated to preach and teach biblical truth, and the truth is that there are times when we can't know when God will intervene and change our situations. And to take that a step further, I have to tell you that there will be times when He *won't* change our situations.

But there is one thing I can tell you with certainty, and it's this: While you are in a place of weakness, pain, grief, trouble, or loss, He will sustain you. He will give you all the grace, mercy, and help you need to get through even the most difficult situations that come your way.

It's human nature to want God to step in and change things during our seasons of trouble. We want that kind of help the very minute we call on Him. But the old saying "Prayer changes *things*" isn't always true. When we step up to the throne of grace, there will be times when God changes our situation, but there also will be times when He allows us to continue in our weakness and difficulty.

If you enjoyed these studies from Tony Evans and desire to purchase your own copy of *God, Do You Really Care?* to read and study in greater detail, visit the LifeWay Christian Store serving you. Or you can order a copy by calling 1-800-233-1123.

Describe in the margin a time when God allowed you to continue "in weakness and difficulty." What did you experience as you went through this season?

_____

Either way, God will put action behind His sympathy. He's won't just say, "I care when you are weak or hurting, and I hope you get through it." God cares more than we can comprehend when we are in the middle of difficult times, and we can rest in His ironclad promise that He will give us the help we need to endure.

Oh yes, God cares, and He has given us a private place to meet with Him when we need His help. It's called His throne of grace, and we can bring anything—big or small—to Him, knowing that the very least He's going to do is give us the help we need to not only endure but to grow and thrive in our faith.

That, my friend, shows us just how very much He cares!

Knowing how much God cares, it is time to bring your issues—big or small—to Him. Make a list in the margin of your issues. Approach the throne of grace boldly. Begin praying over your list, knowing that God specifically cares for your every need.

leader Guide

Before the Session

1. Review the highpoints of each week's study in these eight sessions.
2. Prepare a poster board (or marker board) for use under During the Session Step 8 below. You will use this board to facilitate a list of points summarizing what learners encountered through this *MasterWork* series *God, Do You Really Care?*

During the Session

1. Ask a volunteer to read aloud Hebrews 4:14-16. After this passage is read, ask learners to share how they responded to the interactives at the end of Day 1 on page 90. Explain that we need to remember over and over that Jesus does care when His people suffer. Emphasize that the Letter to the Hebrews was written to Christians who were facing persecution. They needed to know God cared for them.

2. Ask learners how they responded to the interactives on the top of page 92. Ask: *How was Jesus acting as a High Priest in Lazarus's situation? How has Jesus served as a High Priest in your own spiritual journey?* Allow time for discussion. As you explain the nature of Jesus as a High Priest, emphasize that Jesus is literally our access into the heart of God our Father. He has given us complete access. Ask: *When you think about facing challenges in your life, how does it make you feel to know that you have direct access to God when hard times come?*

3. Ask a volunteer to share the illustration about Abraham Lincoln on page 92. Ask learners to share how they responded to the interactive on page 92 that follows this illustration about Abraham Lincoln. Ask: *If you were trying to explain to someone the significance of having full access to God, how would you do it? Can you think of any creative illustrations you would use to emphasize what this means?* Allow time for discussion.

4. Explain that it is all too easy to want to quit. Living our faith in this world is hard stuff. Ask learners to share how they responded to the interactives on page 93.

5. Ask: *What does it mean to you when Dr. Evans wrote: "He understands what we're going through because He's been there Himself"?* Allow time

To the Leader:

The fact that God cares is an amazing truth. Use this lesson to affirm what all eight lessons have emphasized— God cares more than we can imagine. We must trust Him with our difficult situations. We must trust Him to be faithful to keep His promises to us. This lesson will reveal how intimately Jesus cares for us as we walk through each and every day of life.

for responses. Ask learners to share how they responded to the first interactive of Day 4 on page 94.

6. Ask a volunteer to read aloud 2 Corinthians 5:21. Ask: *What does it mean to say that Jesus became sin for us?* Allow learners time to share their thoughts. Then refer to the interactive on page 95. Explain that because God understands our struggles with sin, we can feel safe in approaching Him. Ask learners how they responded to the last interactive of Day 4 on page 96. Allow time for discussion.

7. Ask: *How do you define the word* grace? Ask someone to reread Hebrews 4:14-16 aloud. Ask: *How is grace defined in this passage?* Refer to the first interactive of Day 5 on page 97. Encourage learners to share their personal needs. Review with learners the discussion regarding God working in the midst of our weaknesses and difficulties. Ask learners to share how they responded to the first interactive on page 98.

8. Review with learners the highpoints of each week's study. Ask: *Based on this total study of John 11 and other Scriptures mentioned by Tony Evans, what did you personally learn about the way God cares for us as we walk through hard times?* Use a poster board to allow learners to list the things they learned from this series.

9. As a concluding exercise, use the last interactive of Day 5 on page 98 to guide your learners through a time of prayer and commitment.

ABOUT THE WRITERS

Priscilla Shirer

is a Bible teacher. She is a graduate of the University of Houston, with a Bachelor's degree in Communications, and Dallas Theological Seminary, with a Master's degree in Biblical Studies. For over 10 years Priscilla has been a conference speaker for major corporations, organizations, and Christian audiences across the United States and the world. She is now in full-time ministry to women. Her ministry is focused on the expository teaching of the Word of God. She desires to see women not only know the uncompromising truths of Scripture intellectually but experience them practically by the power of the Holy Spirit.

Priscilla is the daughter of pastor, speaker, and well-known author Dr. Tony Evans. She is married to her best friend, Jerry. The couple have two sons, Jackson and Jerry Jr.

AMY SUMMERS wrote the teaching plans for this study. Amy is a graduate of Baylor University and Southwestern Baptist Theological Seminary.

ABOUT THIS STUDY

Do you believe God *wants* to speak to you? _____

What do you think you could do to better prepare yourself to hear God's voice?

_____

_____

He Speaks to Me

Many believers have become satisfied with a mediocre Christian existence that sits on the sidelines while those we consider more spiritual have a relationship with God. This shouldn't satisfy us. God wants us to hear His voice, understand, and obey.

Could our inability to hear God have less to do with His desire to speak and more to do with our lack of preparedness to hear? The Lord speaks clearly, but those most likely to hear are those who have correctly positioned themselves. While we are waiting on God to do His part, He could be waiting on us to do ours!

This study focuses on what we need to do to prepare ourselves to hear God when He chooses to speak. In 1 Samuel 3 we find a young man who grew up surrounded by religious activity. I can relate to that. Yet the difference between Samuel and me was that He heard God's voice. For much of my Christian life, I didn't! I began a journey to discover the characteristics God must have seen in Samuel that made Him desire to speak and made Samuel capable of hearing. Those six characteristics will unfold over the next six weeks as we look at several individuals who heard God's voice.

God is going to reveal His plan for you in new ways. Make a commitment to be obedient to whatever He says. The results will be glorious!

Priscilla Shirer

A Simple Relationship

day One

A Simple Obedience

After my son Jackson's quiet time yesterday, I asked him to clean up his play area. He bounded to his feet and quickly put everything in its proper place. When he finished, I opened my arms to him, and said, "Come here, sweetie." But my instruction seemed to repel him. He ran from me!

I marveled that he had easily made the effort to clean up his play area, but he fought against the simple obedience required to come to me. Then I thought, How like our relationship to God. We often run from God's request for our attention. We struggle against God's desire that we simply spend time with Him. Why is it sometimes difficult for us to follow the simple instructions the Lord gives us?

THE BASICS OF OBEDIENCE

In Matthew 18 Jesus used a child's willingness to obey to illustrate the beauty of simple obedience. For three years Jesus had been teaching and preaching. His disciples saw Him heal, watched Him feed five thousand, and even saw Him walk on water! So why did the great teacher and miracle worker use a little one to show adults what true obedience looks like? Jesus called and the child came.

Read Matthew 11:20, printed in the margin. Underline how some responded to Jesus' teaching and miracles.

Which of the following best describes how you normally respond to Christ's Word?
❑ rebel   ❑ immediately obey   ❑ question
❑ run away   ❑ argue with God   ❑ other

DIGITAL VIDEO 🖥

If you would be interested in watching Priscilla Shirer herself discuss the material in this *MasterWork* lesson—and more— go to *www.lifeway.com* and purchase your personal copy of the digital video for Session 1 of *He Speaks to Me*.

"Now the boy Samuel ... "
(1 Sam. 3:1, NASB).

Samuel was a child.

Daily Bread
"He called a child to Him" (Matt. 18:2).

"Then He proceeded to denounce the towns where most of His miracles were done, because they did not repent" (Matt. 11:20).

Children have traits that create the openness and willingness the Lord wants adults to recapture. They are naturally curious, using their curiosity to learn. They are excited by learning something new and delight in discovering new truths. That childish excitement points to pure faith and total trust. The Lord wants us to regain these childhood traits. We must repent for the times we have ignored, fought against, or criticized His instructions.

THE SACRIFICE OF OBEDIENCE

Unfortunately, balking against the Lord's instructions often seems easier than following them because obedience requires sacrifice. Here is a list of simple ways the Lord has asked me to obey Him. To fulfill those, I must make some sacrifices.

- To serve my family, I must often forfeit my own desires.
- To spend time with Him regularly, I must say no to other activities.
- To control my eating, I must not overindulge.
- To control my spending, I must not buy every outfit that turns my head.
- To honor my husband's authority, I must release the desire to be in control.

Sacrifices often feel like I am giving up something valuable. I have to remind myself that joy and freedom always lie in obedience. Each of the sacrifices in my list ultimately results in my good. Each of the issues I surrender really contain poison that, if kept, will kill the wonderful future God has for me. Look in the margin to discover how wonderfully author Eugene Peterson expressed this idea in Romans 6:1 in *The Message*.

"You know well enough from your own experience that there are some acts of so-called freedom that destroy freedom. Offer yourselves to sin, for instance, and it's your last free act. But offer yourselves to the ways of God and the freedom never quits" (Rom. 6:1, The Message).

In the margin list steps of simple obedience the Lord is requiring of you in this season of your life. Make a note of the sacrifices you are currently making in obedience to the Lord.

Obedience will not always be easy, but it will always be worth it. Obedience to God always brings reward.

Consider the obedience of the following men. Look up the first passage and note the sacrifice the individuals made by walking obediently with God. Look up the second passage and describe how each was rewarded.

Abraham
Genesis 22:1-3 _____

Genesis 22:16-18 _____

Peter and the apostles
Acts 5:17-29,40 _____

Acts 5:40-42 _____

Remember the example of the little boy in Matthew 18? Jesus chose the child to illustrate simple obedience. By following the Lord in obedience, we are preparing or positioning ourselves to hear His voice. By sacrificing our own desires for His, we are aligning ourselves with His will and opening the door to receive His blessings.

day Two

A Simple Beginning

Through this study our desire is to prepare ourselves to hear God's voice and receive wisdom from Him. Proverbs 1:7 and 9:10, found in the margin, respond to that need.

In the Hebrew of Proverbs 1:7, "the fear" is *Yir' ah*, meaning "to reverence or respect." "Beginning" translates *re' shiyth*, which means "the essence." And "knowledge," *da'ath* in Hebrew, means "perception, discernment, spiritual understanding." I paraphrase this verse as "Respect for the Lord is the essence of spiritual understanding." Showing God respect opens our hearts and our spiritual ears to clearly hear from Him.

In Proverbs 9:10 the word "beginning" is taken from the Hebrew word *ta'chilliah*, which means "the prerequisite, starting point." "Wisdom" in this passage comes from the Hebrew term *chokmah*, which means "skillful, wisdom, wisely." In our quest to hear God's voice, we cannot gain spiritual insight or wisdom if we begin at the wrong place. Our desire to hear from

"The fear of the LORD is the beginning of knowledge" (Prov. 1:7).

"The fear of the LORD is the beginning of wisdom" (Prov. 9:10).

God must begin with reverence. Respecting God is not only the essence of wisdom, it is also the prerequisite for it.

SPIRITUAL WISDOM

Notice the progression: Proverbs 1:7 promises spiritual understanding as a result of respecting God, while Proverbs 9:10 goes further by saying that we also will acquire wisdom. Fearing God not only opens the door to spiritual insight (knowledge) but also allows us to usefully and skillfully apply that insight so it transforms our lives practically. After all, what good is knowledge if we don't know how to apply it?

Fearing God does not mean that we should feel terror but reverence for God's majesty and respect of His power. Our ability to obtain wisdom from God begins and grows with our ability and willingness to fear Him.

Write your own paraphrase of Ecclesiastes 12:13 in the margin.

PRACTICAL RESPECT

As a child, when I was disobedient, I remember my parents saying, "You don't respect me the way you should because if you did you would obey me." When we see God and respect Him for who He is, an attitude of submission and obedience should stem from our desire to honor Him.

What does your current level of practical obedience reveal about your respect for God? Most often I give God:

Little respect		**Conditional respect**		**Total respect**

We wait for God to speak, but have we prepared to hear from Him? Are we reverencing, respecting, and obeying Him? Without the proper preparation, we cannot gain the knowledge and wisdom He provides.

Read Romans 1:21-22, printed in the margin. Circle the phrases that tell what happens when people who have only a head knowledge of God refuse to honor Him.

"For though they knew God, they did not glorify Him as God or show gratitude. Instead, their thinking became nonsense, and their senseless minds were darkened. Claiming to be wise, they became fools" (Rom. 1:21-22).

Intellectual knowledge can help us know about God. But only an intimate, personal relationship leads us to respect, honor, and reverence God. Honoring God is key to hearing from God. Our ability to hear His voice begins when we reverence Him through simple obedience. Knowing God is not enough; we must fear and obey Him.

A Simple Humility

Growing up as the preacher's kid, I became used to church members catering to and taking care of me. The members meant well, but their good intentions created problems for me as I became an adult. I constantly have to work on humility, consciously striving to consider others before myself. But I know I am not alone in my struggle to remain humble.

Just before Jesus called to the young child, a conflict arose among the disciples. In Matthew 18:1 we find, "At that time the disciples came to Jesus and said, 'Who is the greatest in the kingdom of heaven?' " On the heels of this argument Jesus told the disciples to humble themselves like a child.

In what areas of your life do you face similar conflict?
❑ **marriage** ❑ **work** ❑ **family** ❑ **neighborhood**
❑ **school** ❑ **church** ❑ **other:**_____

WHAT IS HUMILITY?
A truly humble person does not deny the gifts God has given her nor brag about them as if they are by her own doing. Humility is the ability to think of others, putting their needs before your own.

List three people you know who demonstrate humility. Record your thoughts about how humility is evidenced by their actions. _____

_____

Take Action
Ask the Lord to forgive you for any rebellion against His instructions. List some specific areas in which you desire to more closely obey the Lord. Pick one and list steps you can take today to walk in obedience in that area.

Daily Bread
"Whoever humbles himself like this child—this one is the greatest in the kingdom of heaven" (Matt. 18:4).

The sin of pride was the obvious catalyst for the disciples' argument. What happened just before the disciples argued over which of them would be greatest in the kingdom indicates this. Jesus revealed His impending death in Luke 9:44-45.

How did the disciples respond to His news?

_____

The disciples overlooked the message of Christ's impending death because they were too concerned with themselves to concentrate on His words. Pride is a distraction. Often Jesus wants to reveal important information to us, but our prideful hearts get in the way of our ability to hear the message. Humility clears the pathway for us to hear God.

Humility should be the natural outpouring of hearts grateful to the Lord. When we consider all the King has done for us, given us, and forgiven us, our hearts should be overjoyed. We should humbly submit to Him like children gratefully submitting to a loving parent.

day Four

A Simple Trust

As we become adults, life experiences often can lead to difficulty in trusting. We become more self-sufficient. Yet Jesus desires that we approach Him with *total* trust and believe in Him with the simplicity of a child. It takes more than humility to respond to God; it takes trust. In Matthew 18:6, Christ used the Greek word *pisteuo* to refer to the child's belief. It means "to think to be true, to place complete confidence in." We have to ask, "What happens between childhood and adulthood that causes children and adults to respond differently to God?"

How has your faith in the Lord changed since you first entered into a relationship with Him and why?

_____

THE CONSEQUENCE OF UNBELIEF

Numbers 20:8-12 demonstrates Moses' lack of faith in God's instructions. In verse 8 God specifically instructed Moses to "speak to the rock."

How did Moses disobey? _____

What consequences did he have to face as a result?

_____

Notice God's reprimand came not for simply disobeying but rather for not believing God. Failure to do exactly what God asks, regardless of how strange or incomplete His instructions seem, shows lack of faith in God Himself. By not doing what He tells us, we are saying that we don't trust that God is wise enough or capable enough to handle our situation.

Take Action

Rewrite Matthew 21:22 in your own words.

Recall a time you received instructions from God that seemed strange and you didn't want to follow. What happened as a result of your action or inaction? Write your answer in the margin.

In Numbers 20 Moses did not follow God's instructions, but by God's grace, the people received the water they needed. Moses and Aaron, however, still suffered the consequences of unbelief. Moses prayed that he and the others would see the land God promised, but his request was not fulfilled because he failed to trust God.

The following verses show the importance of faith in our relationship to God. Write key words beside each.

Isaiah 7:9 _____

John 3:18 _____

John 8:24 _____

Hebrews 3:12 _____

Could the cause of our unanswered prayers be our lack of childlike pisteuo [faith]? Ask God to show you when you are not obeying His instructions, thinking instead that your way is better than His. Thank Him for His continued grace, and admit the areas where you lack full trust in His instructions.

A Simple Dependence

Daily Bread

"LORD, my heart is not proud; my eyes are not haughty. I do not get involved with things too great or too difficult for me. Instead, I have calmed and quieted myself like a little weaned child with its mother; I am like a little child" (Ps. 131:1-2).

This week we have explored the basics of placing ourselves in a position to hear from God: being obedient, fearing the Lord, obtaining wisdom, remaining humble, and trusting God's plans above our own. In Psalm 131:1-2 David described another important basic—dependence on God. David began his conversation with God by confessing his inadequacy. This powerful man who would soon be king didn't credit himself for the blessings in his life (see 1 Sam. 16:1-12; 17:45-50). He formed a deeper dependence on God, trusting in Him as a child trusts a loving parent.

Circle your level of dependence on God: 5 being the highest level and 1 being the lowest.

Finances	1	2	3	4	5
Family	1	2	3	4	5
Marriage	1	2	3	4	5
Parenting	1	2	3	4	5
Career	1	2	3	4	5

As a speaker and Bible teacher, I've learned to be careful not to rely on my communication skills or familiarity with the message. When I rely on familiarity rather than relying on the power of the Holy Spirit, the message lacks power and anointing. On the other hand, when I depend on the Lord and confess my inadequacy, He touches hearts in ways I never could.

Read Psalm 131:1-2, printed in the margin, and circle the things David declared he had done.

THE CALMED SOUL

First David said, "I have calmed … myself." Calming is an action of which David had to take control. He compared it to weaning a child. I can tell you from experience that weaning takes discipline! Calming your soul into a state of dependence on God also requires discipline. Just as a mother has to discipline herself to offer her child a cup when weaning, so too must you direct yourself to the nourishment of the Lord when your soul cries out for its old dependencies. Our natural tendency is to trust our own ambitions, gifts, talents, abilities and earthly wisdom to make decisions. However, if you remain faithful to Him, sooner or later you will find nothing else will satisfy.

THE QUIETED SOUL

Weaning requires a season of discomfort. When we begin to wean ourselves of dependence on other things, we may feel uneasy, fretful, and un-comfortable. But without the crutch of dependence on ourselves or others, it becomes easier to turn to God for comfort and spiritual nourishment.

Read Psalm 42:5-6, written when David's soul was in a state of unrest during the "weaning" process. What did David say is the solution to calming one's soul?

_____

David quieted his soul by remembering what God had done. The more you trust your concerns to the Lord and see Him working in your life, the more willing you will be to depend on Him in the future.

THE RESTED SOUL

His soul calmed and quieted, David pointed out the final step of the process—rest. A weaned baby no longer desires milk from his mother. He knows it comes from the refrigerator. He rests in his new situation. So too our souls will reorient themselves to a new way of feeding as we accept God alone for refreshment.

If we seek fulfillment in the things of the world after a season of depending on God, we will discover that it doesn't satisfy us the way it used to. When we are thirsty, we need so much more than the world can offer. But hallelujah, God never disappoints!

Take Action

Circle the category in the dependence activity on page 110 in which you've made the greatest progress trusting God in the past year. Pause to thank God for the areas where you've grown.

What has God done in your life that can build trust when you struggle to depend on Him?

On what people, places, or ambitions do you tend to depend more for satisfaction than on the Lord?

Ask for the Lord's assistance in depending on Him in situations you are currently facing. Allow Him an opportunity to win your trust.

NOTES

Before the Session

If you choose the option in Step 1, provide three placards labeled "True," "False," and "Not Sure" and tape for displaying.

During the Session

1. Ask: *Do you think God speaks to all Christians or just a few select "spiritual giants"? Why don't we always hear God speak?* OR Instruct learners to answer "True," "False," or "Not Sure" after you read each of the following statements: *1. God speaks to me. 2. I always hear when God speaks to me. 3. I want to hear when God speaks to me.* (OPTION: Display "True," "False," or "Not Sure" placards around the room and direct learners to stand next to the placard that best reflects their response to each statement.) FOR EITHER OPTION: Declare that in this six-week study learners will discover characteristics that prepared the prophet Samuel to hear God, examine those characteristics in-depth, and strive to incorporate them in their own lives so they hear God when He speaks.

2. Request learners state the first thing 1 Samuel 3:1 reveals about Samuel. [He was a child.] Ask: *Are children's relationships simple or complicated? Why?* Declare: *To be in a position to hear God when He speaks, we need the simplicity of a child.* Determine childish traits Christ wants adults to recapture and why those help us hear Him speak. Ask: *Why do we balk at obeying the Lord?* Lead learners to look at Priscilla Shirer's list on page 104 and add sacrifices that believers must make to obey God's instructions. Ask: *What makes these sacrifices worth it?* Read Matthew 18:2-4 and consider sacrifices the child had to make to obey Jesus and the resulting rewards. [Sample: It was scary to stand in front of those men. Maybe he had to quit playing, but how awesome to be the focus of Jesus' attention and commendation!] Urge learners to relate with God through practical obedience.

3. Encourage learners to state basics of solid relationships. Declare all good relationships begin with mutual respect. Request someone read Proverbs 1:7. Use Priscilla's comments in Day 2 (p. 105) to examine the concept of fearing God. Inquire: *In Day 2, according to the last two*

To the Leader:

Each teaching plan for this six-week study will provide two options for beginning the session. The first option is a basic discussion-opener question. The second option will involve a little more interaction. The best option is to let both ideas spur your own creativity to begin each class session in a way that captures learners' interest so they are eager to discuss and digest God's Word.

words of both proverbs on page 105, what does respecting and reverencing God lead to? What's the difference in these two terms? Allow volunteers to share their paraphrase of Ecclesiastes 12:13 (p. 106). Request learners silently consider the personal evaluation activity about their respect for God. Read Priscilla's comments ("We wait for God to speak...") following that activity.

4. Request someone read Matthew 18:4. Consider why simple humility is a desirable characteristic in any relationship. Request a volunteer read Exodus 3:11. Determine why that attitude does not describe true humility. Invite learners to identify the phrase in Romans 12:3 that does not describe humility. Ask: *Why might you not want to spend much time communicating with either of these two types of people? What phrase in Romans 12:3 does define humility? Why could you enjoy relating with that kind of person?* Organize the class into two groups. Request the first group state what they learn about humility from Isaiah 57:15 and 66:2, and the second group do the same with James 4:6,10. Complete the *Take Action* activity in the margin of Day 3 (p. 108).

5. Remark that trust is also basic to all good relationships. Read Priscilla's question at the end of the first paragraph of Day 4 (p. 108). Request adults silently consider the question in boldface type. Guide adults to discover from Hebrews 11:6 why trust is essential to hear from God. Ask what results from trusting God. Comment that not trusting God also has results. Discuss the questions related to Numbers 20:8-12 (p. 109). Ask: *According to verse 12, why was God so upset with Moses' actions? How do our actions reveal whether we trust God? How can we become Christians who trust God enough?*

6. Ask learners to state from Psalm 131:1-2 the final basic characteristic for hearing from God. Ask what David did to express his dependence on God. Discuss the Psalm 42:5-6 activity in Day 5 (p. 111). Ask: *How well do you listen to others when you're hurried and harried? When you're calm, quiet, and rested? So what's the logical conclusion if we want to hear God?* Invite learners to consider the *Take Action* suggestions in the margin on page 111 and share their responses.

7. Urge learners to follow Samuel's example and relate to God with childlike simplicity. Encourage them to keep in mind that the child Samuel was a worshiper as they study Week 2. Close in prayer.

A Single-Minded Worship

day One

His Glory

"Now the boy Samuel was ministering to the LORD before Eli ... " (1 Sam. 3:1, NASB).

Samuel was a worshiper.

Daily Bread

"The appearance of the LORD's glory to the Israelites was like a consuming fire on the mountaintop" (Ex. 24:17).

• God's glory is all around us, even in the desert places.
• God's glory exceeds comprehension.
• God's glory is reserved for only One.
• God's glory demands a response.

True undistracted worship begins when we concentrate on God's glory. We honor Him by taking the focus off ourselves and training our eyes on Him. God chooses to speak to those focused on His glory. In Exodus 3 an angel of the Lord appeared to Moses in the midst of a blazing bush miraculously unconsumed by flame. Today we'll explore the lessons on glory that I see reflected in the passage. They are summarized in the margin for you.

GOD'S GLORY APPEARS EVEN AND ESPECIALLY IN THE DESERT PLACES

Moses spent his first 40 years as a prince in Pharaoh's court (see Ex. 2:1-10). Yet at the ripe age of 80 he encountered the glory of God in a barren desert. Often we see God's glory best against the contrast of life's dry seasons.

Record in the margin on page 115 how God has used a "wilderness season" to reveal Himself to you.

God's glory discovers us where we are. Shepherding was beneath Moses' educational and economic expectations. But he accepted it and served where he was; then God's glory showed up. Friend, be faithful even in the desert seasons because that's where God's glory often appears.

GOD'S GLORY EXCEEDS COMPREHENSION

The bush, burning yet unconsumed, defied the laws of nature, but Moses soon learned that God's glory is always beyond human understanding. Any attempt to comprehend God's complexities or to liken Him to man minimizes His greatness and power. In Deuteronomy 5:8, God calls human attempts to capture His glory idol-making.

As a matter of contrast to idols, match the Scripture passage below with the appropriate illustration of God's incomparable power.

___ **1 Thessalonians 1:9**   **a. living and true God**
___ **Jeremiah 10:16**   **b. great King; above all gods**
___ **Psalm 95:3**   **c. formed all things**

GOD'S GLORY IS RESERVED FOR ONLY ONE

In a dry, barren desert, Moses may have been amazed not simply because the bush wasn't consumed but because only one bush burned. In this singular burning I see a hint of another important truth: God does not share His glory. Even as Christians, we often desire "glory" in the eyes of man. We want the fire reserved for God to spread to us.

Think of ways you have sought to share in God's glory. What happened when you tried to share the glory reserved for God?

_____

Reflect on Isaiah 48:11 and 2 Thessalonians 2:14, printed in the margin. In what sense do you think God will not share His glory? In what sense does He share? Makes notes in the margin and plan to discuss your answers in your group this week.

"I will act for My own sake, indeed, My own, for how can I be defiled? I will not give My glory to another" (Isa. 48:11).

GOD'S GLORY DEMANDS A RESPONSE

In Exodus 3 we find that when God's glory showed up, Moses stopped his normal duties to respond. The revealed glory of God demands that we pause, listen, and heed His voice. Who knows what we miss when we don't change our plans for His? When we know we are in His presence, we must quickly and reverently adopt three responses found in Moses' response.

"He called you to salvation when we told you the Good News; now you can share in the glory of our Lord Jesus Christ" (2 Thess. 2:14, NLT).

Take Action
When we worship, recognize, and respond to God's glory, we put ourselves in a position for Him to speak. Look carefully at Exodus 3:4. God spoke to Moses only after he "turned aside." How is God calling you to "turn aside" as a result of today's study?
- *Pray the Lord will open your spiritual eyes.*
- *Make a commitment to respond to God's glory whenever you encounter it.*

Daily Bread
"They are to make a sanctuary for Me so that I may dwell among them. You must make it according to all that I show you—the design of the tabernacle as well as the design of all its furnishings" (Ex. 25:8-9).

Read Exodus 3:3-6 and fill in the blanks.

First (vv. 3-4), we must _____ to God. God's glory demands that we come away from whatever we are doing and turn our attention to Him.

Second (v. 5), we must _____ ourselves before Him. Moses acknowledges his unworthiness to stand in the presence of God's holiness.

Third (v. 6), we must _____ our faces from God. Moses wasn't afraid of God. He reacted in reverence and awe of God. We too must bow before God's glory.

day *Two*

His Priorities

Just as we must respond to God's glory to offer Him acceptable worship, we must also focus on His priorities. In Exodus 25–26 God told Moses exactly how to construct a tabernacle of worship. God required it to be built by specific people, who followed specific instructions, for a specific purpose.

A SPECIFIC PEOPLE

In Exodus 25:2 God specifies who will construct His tabernacle. First, they had to be His people (Deut. 7:6). Second, God specified only those "whose hearts are stirred" to participate in this project (Ex. 25:2). God receives worship from His people alone. Acceptable worship of God must be from His children who are willingly present and centered on Him.

Read Romans 8:15. How is our relationship with God similar to that of the children of Israel's?

_____

As sons and daughters of God, we are chosen to live as His children for all eternity. That fact should so overwhelm us with thanksgiving that we long to worship Him.

A SPECIFIC PLAN

In the margin list what you plan ahead of time in a typical week. What does planning reveal about the level of significance you place on these things?

Exodus 25–27 reveals the attention to detail God required of Moses and the Israelites. Imagine the time and patience required to meet each specification for each item. Everything had to be done correctly.

Read Exodus 25:9, printed in the margin. Underline the word that shows how important it was that the people followed God's plans for the tabernacle.

"Make this tabernacle and all its furnishings exactly like the pattern I will show you" (Ex. 25:9, NIV).

God considers preparing for worship important. This doesn't mean that He gives us a specific picture of exactly how that worship should look, as He did in the building of the tabernacle. Instead, He instructs us in how to plan for opportunities to worship Him.

A SPECIFIC PURPOSE

God clearly showed the Israelites a worthy purpose to all of their planning, preparation, and patience. In taking His instructions and priorities seriously, they would be invited into His very presence.

Review the day by filling in the blanks below.

_____ must take place before we can truly worship (1 Sam. 15:25; Ps. 51:2).

We must not worship any other _____ (Ex. 34:14; Ps. 81:9).

We must _____ _____ **in true worship (Ps. 95:6).**

Take Action

How much preparation do you usually put into your worship? Do you "prepare prayerfully" or "just show up"? Ask the Lord to make you a true worshiper. Confess any lack of planning, preparation, or patience. Make a commitment to work on those areas.

day Three

His Attributes

Daily Bread

"I am the God of your father, the God of Abraham, the God of Isaac and the God of Jacob" (Ex. 3:6).

God is ...

- just (Heb. 10:30-31)
- good (Matt. 19:17)
- holy (Rev. 15:4)
- righteous (Ps. 119:137)
- sovereign (Isa. 46:9-10)
- everywhere (Ezek. 48:35)
- all knowing (Heb. 4:13)
- unchanging (Jas. 1:17)
- truth (Isa. 65:16)
- merciful (Eph. 2:4)
- jealous (Ex. 34:14)
- love (1 John 4:8)
- eternal (Isa. 48:12)
- a provider (Gen. 22:14)
- a healer (Ex. 15:26)

To worship God acceptably we must know Him. Understanding God's attributes—the distinguishing marks of His character—will help us grow to appreciate Him in a deeper, more intimate way. Meditating on His attributes helps us move from knowing *about* God to truly *knowing* Him.

In Exodus 3:6 God reminded Moses of His record of faithfulness, so Moses knew he could count on God regardless of circumstances. No matter how you feel or what you experience, God's attributes remain true. That knowledge should drive us to our knees in true worship.

Look at the list in the margin. Circle God's attributes you have seen evidenced in or impacting your life.

WHEN GOD REVEALS HIS ATTRIBUTES

Moses remained dependent on God throughout his service to the Lord. Because he felt ill-equipped (see Ex. 3:11 and 4:10), he never thought he had arrived. Moses remained aware of his own desperate need. In Exodus 33:18 Moses begged God, "Please, let me see Your glory."

Stop and read Exodus 33:19-23 and 34:1-8.

THE POWER OF GOD

When God replaced the broken tablets of the law, He began revealing Himself to Moses by reminding him of His great power (see Ex. 34:5-7). With the people's great sin of creating and worshiping a golden calf (see Ex. 14:9 and 32:7-8) fresh on his mind, Moses likely needed a reminder that God is great enough not only to defeat their enemies but also to forgive their iniquity! God's power and might are so great that they powerfully and fully cleanse us of iniquity.

How does the truth that God can forgive because of His grace and almighty power make you feel?

_____

THE MERCY OF GOD

In Exodus 34:6 we find God revealed His mercy to Moses: "Yahweh is a compassionate and gracious God, slow to anger and rich in faithful love and truth." God reminded Moses of His grace as Moses stood to represent the people of Israel, confess their sins, and seek forgiveness before receiving the second installment of the Ten Commandments. God forgives sin. In the midst of our sin, His mercy steps in and saves us from ourselves.

Why was it important that God showed the attribute of mercy before revealing the law?

_____

_____

THE JUSTICE OF GOD

After establishing His mercy God reveals in Exodus 34:7, that He is a God of truth and judgment: "He will not leave [the guilty] unpunished." Although we know the wonders of His grace and mercy, we must not take His justice lightly.

Understand that sin leads to consequence. God punished the children of Israel. But His grace and mercy provided forgiveness. Although He punished sin, He loved the sinners.

day *Four*

His Acceptance

To worship God appropriately we also need to grasp His acceptance. As long as we feel condemned, we will have difficulty believing God wants

Take Action
Reread Moses' response to the revelation of God's character in Exodus 34:8. Answer the following.

• How quickly did Moses respond?

• What did Moses' external position show about his internal state?

Commentator Matthew Henry says Moses' desire to worship God shows:

1. He humbly revered and adored God.

2. He was joyful and thankful at his discovery of God.

3. He was submissive to the revelation of God's will.[1]

Pray that these three things will be true of you as God reveals His attributes throughout this study.

Daily Bread

"Be careful not to practice your righteousness in front of people, to be seen by them. Otherwise, you will have no reward from your Father in heaven" (Matt. 6:1).

to speak to us. The Lord has to continuously remind me that He loves me, desires intimacy with me, and longs to speak to me.

THE PROBLEM

The Jewish people continuously tried to find perfection following the law and offering sacrifices, but they always came up short. No matter how often the people sacrificed, no matter how closely they tried to follow the law, they remained unacceptable to God.

The problem is a human one. In our own power we will always be inadequate. Only God's sacrifice of His Son for our sin makes us acceptable.

List things you like best about yourself.

_____

Read Isaiah 64:6. Why do the traits you just listed not make you acceptable to God?

_____

We are not made acceptable to God by *who* we are but by *whose* we are. Jesus bridges the gap. Hebrews 10:14 tells us, "For by one offering He has perfected forever those who are sanctified." The word *perfect* here means "perfectly adequate."[2] The death of Jesus on the cross is the only sacrifice ever needed for us to be acceptable and adequate in His sight.

In what ways have you tried following the law to make yourself acceptable to God?

❏ **a moral lifestyle** ❏ **religious activity** ❏ **prayer**
❏ **sacrificial giving** ❏ **confession** ❏ **other** _____

Hear this incredibly liberating truth: You cannot make yourself acceptable to God. Hebrews 10:1-4 explains that the continued offering of bull and goat blood did not take away sins. You can be sure that whatever you are offering will not "perfect" you either.

THE SOLUTION

List things you like least about yourself.

_____

According to Ephesians 2:6, what is our position once we become Christians?

_____

Why does the trait you like least about yourself not keep you from standing righteous before God?

_____

Jesus gives us the right to claim God as Father. By accepting the perfect sacrifice of Jesus for the remission of our sins, we can "have confidence to enter the holy place" (Heb. 10:19, NASB). As Christians, we are completely acceptable to God. Nothing can change our standing before Him!

Take Action

Read Hebrews 4:16. Because God accepts us in Christ, we can approach God's throne with confidence. If you already have a personal relationship with the Lord, spend some time in prayer, thanking Him for your salvation. If you aren't certain you have received God's gift of eternal life, turn to "How to Become a Christian" on the inside of the front cover of this book. Ask someone to explain to you how you can become a Christ-follower.

day Five

His Approval

FOCUSED ON HIS APPROVAL

Read Moses' conversation with God in Exodus 3:10-16. What was Moses' main concern (vv. 10-11,13)?

_____

How did God redirect Moses' attention (vv. 12,14-16)?

_____

Daily Bread

"So Jesus has also become the guarantee of a better covenant" (Heb. 7:22).

Take Action
What has God specifically spoken to you about this week? Write your responses as a prayer.

Here God reveals a final principle about seeking to be single-minded in our worship of Him. God reveals to Moses that he can carry out His instructions only if he takes his eyes off the people and keeps them on God. We must do the same. Our acts must be dedicated to God alone—not to the approval of others.

While external appearance or actions may consume us, our internal motivation concerns God. Have you every done something "religious" to satisfy people more than to please God? Appearing to be holy has no kingdom value. Jesus spoke harshly to a group of Pharisees about this.

Read Jesus' words in Matthew 23:23-29.

How does it feel to be clean on the outside but dirty on the inside? We need to take inventory of our hearts to make sure the motives behind our actions are pure. God responds to those who seek Him with their whole hearts. Ask the Lord to help you offer the authentic worship He desires.

THE HEART OF THE MATTER

To be single-minded in our search for God, our hearts cannot be caught up in details that steal attention from Him.

Write at least one thing you can do to focus on each area we've considered this week:

His glory _____

After talking to the Lord about your goals, write today's date at the top of the page to remind you of your renewed commitment to focus on Him in worship.

His priorities _____

His attributes _____

His acceptance _____

His approval _____

[1] Matthew Henry, *Matthew Henry's Commentary on the Whole Bible* (Peabody: Hendrickson, 1996), electronic ed.
[2] *New International Version Disciple's Study Bible* (Nashville: Holman Bible Publishers, 1998), 1587.

Before the Session

Provide a whiteboard and markers to be used throughout the session.

During the Session

1. Say: *Describe a single-minded person. Do you think that type of focused person is more often successful or unsuccessful in life? Why?* OR Organize the class into groups of three or four. [If the class is co-ed, groups of men and women would be interesting!] Instruct groups to list things they can do while doing something else simultaneously. Then direct them to list actions that require their undivided attention. FOR EITHER OPTION: Declare that hearing God speak requires a single-minded worship. Instruct learners to discover what Samuel was doing in 1 Samuel 1:28 and 3:1. Ask someone to read the first paragraph of Day 1 (p. 114).

2. Invite a volunteer to read Exodus 3:1-6. Ask: *Where was Moses and what was he doing when God's glory appeared? What does that say to you?* Discuss what Moses discovered about God's glory when the bush burned but didn't burn up. Explore what people have done in their attempt to comprehend and control God's glory (see the activity at the top of p. 115). Ask someone to read Romans 1:21-25. Discuss what happens when people refuse to glorify God and how God responds to their attempts to "humanize" Him. Encourage adults to share their thoughts from the last activity on page 115. Determine different ways people respond to God's glory. Complete the final activity of Day 1 to learn from Moses the proper response to God's glory [look, humble, hide]. Analyze the relationship between these responses and hearing God speak. Invite someone to read the *Take Action* in the margin of page 116. Discuss what it means for believers to "turn aside."

3. Declare that single-minded worship requires the proper response to God's glory and a focus on His priorities. Ask: *Who does God intend to worship Him?* Discuss both activities under "A Specific Plan" (p. 117). Instruct the class to listen for God's purpose for the tabernacle as you read aloud Exodus 25:8,22. Ask: *What is God's specific purpose for worship? Will this happen by accident or does it require preparation? Explain.* Declare that if

To the Leader:

Ponder 1 Samuel 1:28 and 3:1. As an adult Bible study leader, do you separate your ministry to the Lord from your worship of the Lord? Ask God to help you focus on His priorities so your ministry to your Sunday School class becomes a form of single-minded worship of Him.

we want God to speak to us we must prepare to focus on His priorities. Ask: *How can we as individuals and a class prepare to worship God?* Use the final activity of Day 2 (p. 117) to help answer that question.

4. State that a single-minded worshiper knows God intimately by knowing and experiencing His attributes. Allow volunteers to share their responses to the first activity in Day 3. Read aloud Daniel 11:32b. Ask learners how they have observed that truth. Explain that Moses never felt strong in himself and remained desperately aware of his need for God's power. Ask a volunteer to read aloud Exodus 33:18-23. List God's attributes mentioned in this passage. After God revealed His glory to Moses, He reminded him of His great power. Read Exodus 34:1-8 and discuss what can be learned about God's power from that passage. Discuss the activity under "The Power of God" (p. 118) and the questions under *Take Action* in the margin (p. 119). Examine how knowing and worshiping God for His attributes puts believers in a position to hear Him when He speaks.

5. Ask why Mrs. Shirer would declare that we need to grasp God's acceptance of us if we are to worship Him appropriately. To determine humanity's problem, ask learners to silently list things they like about themselves. Together discuss the question related to Isaiah 64:6 (p. 120). Next direct learners to silently list what they least like about themselves. Read aloud Ephesians 2:6-9 and guide learners to discuss the last two questions in Day 4 (p. 121). Ask: *Why is the truth that we cannot make ourselves acceptable to God actually good news instead of a problem?* State that God has made us acceptable through Christ's sacrifice. Instruct learners to turn to the inside front cover of *MasterWork* and follow along as you explain how people can accept Christ's solution to their problem. Urge anyone who would like to receive Christ to speak with you after the session.

6. State: *When God looks on us and sees Christ, we have His approval and can worship Him freely and joyfully.* Discuss the opening questions of Day 5 (p. 121). Ask what Mrs. Shirer said is the final principle in seeking to worship God single-mindedly [focus on His approval]. Read aloud Matthew 23:23-29. Discuss whether or not the Pharisees had Christ's approval. Ask: *How can we be clean and genuinely devoted to God inside and out?* Read aloud Deuteronomy 4:29 to help answer that question. Use the final activity of Day 5 to review the week's study. Close in prayer.

A Set-Apart Holiness

day One

Dead to Sin

In 2001 I met "Grandfather," a savage Indian man who participated in the killings of Jim Elliot and other missionaries in Ecuador. My life was impacted forever. He shared how drastically his life had changed. Now he and his tribesmen were serving Christ, living a life that spoke of their new identity in the Lord. He was shocked at how American Christians seem to so closely resemble the rest of society. He was dismayed that we don't seem to live in a way that clearly shows we serve a different God.

We must choose to live a lifestyle of *sanctification* that sets us apart from the world and speaks of a relationship with our great God. As Christians we are sanctified—set apart or made holy. Positionally this process was accomplished by the sacrifice of Christ on the cross. When we enter into a personal relationship with Jesus, the punishment for our sins has already been covered by His death and resurrection.

Our responsibility is to actively pursue holy lives (1 Pet. 1:15). We are set apart by God for His purposes, and everything we do reflects on Him. As believers we've been born into the family of God, and His family name has a holy reputation. We can never perfectly uphold our divine family name on our own strength, but we can live as set apart vessels—no longer enslaved to sin—through God's power.

Since your salvation, what signs do you see that your desires have changed? List them in the margin. Plan to talk about these signs in your group this week.

In what specific areas might you still be living as a slave to sin? List these in the margin as well.

DIGITAL VIDEO 🖥

If you would be interested in watching Priscilla Shirer herself discuss the material in this *MasterWork* lesson—and more— go to *www.lifeway.com* and purchase your personal copy of the digital video for Session 3 of *He Speaks to Me*.

"And word from the LORD was rare in those days, visions were infrequent" (1 Sam. 3:1, NASB).

Samuel was set apart.

Daily Bread

"We know that our old self was crucified with Him in order that sin's dominion over the body may be abolished, so that we may no longer be enslaved to sin, since a person who has died is freed from sin's claims" (Rom. 6:6-7).

125

THE PROCESS OF DYING TO SIN

Though as children of God we are no longer enslaved by sin, ignoring it and avoiding its allure remains a challenge—especially when a sin has become a satisfying habit.

Read 1 Corinthians 15:31-34. According to verse 31, how often did Paul find it necessary to die to his flesh? _____

As Christians we have a responsibility to *daily* let go of those things that distract us from our relationship with the Lord. For me, gluttony is a sin with which I struggle constantly. I love to eat! I am not one of those women content to order a nice, petite salad. I will not only devour my meal of meat and potatoes but I'll scan your plate for leftovers.

Each day I must die to my desire to eat more than I need. I know this will ultimately make me a better example of how God's children should live. As I get more into the habit of sacrificing my selfish desires, it becomes easier. But I suspect that gluttony will always be a struggle for me. I must remember that self-control strengthens my Christian witness.

Note in the margin the sins you have to crucify daily.

Take Action

Read Romans 6:12-13. Notice that the words let, obey, and offer are actions that require a choice. We must ask ourselves to what will we yield. To our flesh or to our new nature? End today's study with prayer time. Ask God to sanctify every area of your life and to give you the strength to die to self and yield to Him.

TRUE FREEDOM

The world's definition of freedom often means the right to openly rebel against God. But that kind of freedom can bring a heavy price. Sexual freedom leads to guilt, sickness, fear, and unwanted pregnancy. Gossip leads to distrust and broken relationships. In every case, the world's freedom ultimately leads to emptiness and despair.

God offers freedom that leads to abundance and peace. A life yielded to Him results in the fruit of the Spirit (see Gal. 5:22-23). As Christians, we must make decisions and choices that will lead us to live lives set apart for Him.

Read Galatians 5:1 aloud twice using the personal pronoun "me." Write it on a card and post it in a place where you will see it often.

day Two

Alive in Christ

Daily Bread

"I pray that the eyes of your heart may be enlightened so you may know what is the hope of His calling, what are the glorious riches of His inheritance among the saints and what is the surpassing greatness of His power toward us who believe. These are in accordance with the working of the strength of His might which He brought about in Christ, when He raised Him from the dead and seated Him at His right hand in the heavenly places" (Eph. 1:18-20, NASB).

Have you ever wished you could run into a phone booth and come out with the superhero power to meet the demands of life? God has provided something even better for Christians. Romans 6:5 says that since we have been united with Christ in His death, we can be assured that the same power that raised Him from the dead is available to us. In Philippians 3:10 Paul wrote that one of his greatest aspirations was to actively *know* the power of Christ's resurrection, using it to live free of sin's grip. We can live a sanctified life because we have divine power.

Yesterday we discussed the importance of daily dying to sin. But lifestyle sanctification doesn't stop there. We must be set apart *from* one thing and set apart *to* something else. Consider what Paul said in Colossians.

List what Colossians 3:8,12-14 tells Christ's followers to *put off* and what to *put on*.

Put Off	*Put On*

Put an X by the items most difficult for you to put off. Put a check by the items most difficult to put on.

Paul knew his request was not easy. That's why in Ephesians 1:18 he prayed that we will know that our position as God's children means more than just salvation from sin. We receive an incomparable power, a superhuman power, and an overcoming power.

AN INCOMPARABLE POWER

In Ephesians 1:19 Paul described the power at work in believers with a three-word Greek phrase: *hyperballo megethos dunamis*. The *New International Version* translates them: "incomparably great power."

The power to live righteously comes from the Holy Spirit living in you, giving you the power to live a sanctified life. Humility, forgiveness, gentleness, and patience: these are indeed impossibilities in your own strength. Without allowing the Holy Spirit to daily work in your life, you cannot be patient on your job or with your family. You cannot put aside anger and resentment when you feel they are deserved.

In the margin, describe a challenge you face without the Spirit's power. Then describe the difference the Spirit's power makes in your life. See the example.

A SUPERHUMAN POWER

The second phrase in Ephesians 1:19, which begs further study, is "the working." The Greek word for "working" is *energien,* meaning "energetic power."[1] Scripture uses *energien* only to reference superhuman power. While *dunamis* power comes from the indwelling of the Holy Spirit, the superhuman phenomenon *energien* is the energy to get us up and into action so this great power can be used.

Which is more difficult for you?
❏ **believe God has given you the power to serve Him**
❏ **actually get up and do what God calls you to do**

Do you currently lack the spiritual energy required to accomplish something God asks of you?
❏ **Yes**   ❏ **No**   ❏ **I'm not sure**
If yes, briefly describe the situation.

AN OVERCOMING POWER

In Ephesians 1:19, the third phrase that we must give attention to is "the strength of His might." The Greek word for "strength" here is *kratos.* It means "power that overcomes resistance" or "dominion" and is used only of God, never of humans. The Greek word used for "might" is *ischus,* meaning "powerful ability." Interestingly, this is the same power that God used to take dominion over death. This same power helps us overcome sin in our lives.

The apostle Paul realized that Christians would lack the ability to live for Christ, so he reminded us that the power available to us comes through God's strength—not our own. We have no excuse not to put on righteousness. We must ask God to help us live sanctified lives through His dynamic and divine power.

Remember, *sanctification* means dying to sin, but it also means living to Christ. We will always struggle with sin in this life. However, we can put on Christ, allowing His power to flow through us, His energy to motivate us, and His strength to rule over and through us. In one sense we have put on Christ once-for-all. In another sense we must put on Christ daily.

Take Action

Pretend you are explaining Philippians 2:13 to a friend. What would you say about the source of our power to serve Christ? Write your response, including the concepts of dunamis, energien, and kratos.

day Three

A Firm Decision

I suspect most of us would like to "cut corners" when it comes to living a sanctified life. Subconsciously we ask ourselves, "What can I do to 'just get by' as a Christian?" In Joshua 24, Joshua called the people to make a clear choice between serving other gods or serving the Lord. Let's see if the process Joshua described can help us with the struggle to lead a life without compromise.

INCENTIVES FOR COMMITMENT

When Joshua challenged the people, he began by gathering the people at Shechem, the place where God had promised to give the land to Abram's offspring. Often, in order to get our attention, God takes us back to a place where He made a promise to us, showed us His power, or revealed Himself to us. He may even take us back to a painful place, using it to remind us to serve Him wholeheartedly. In this sense, we all have our "Shechems."

Your Shechem may not be a physical location but an emotional or mental state. For instance, the Lord might remind you of a painful relationship in your past. He shows you again how that relationship affected you and the decisions you made as a result. Going back to this place reminds you of His goodness, grace, and power.

Daily Bread

"If it doesn't please you to worship the LORD, choose for yourselves today the one you will worship: the gods your fathers worshiped beyond the Euphrates River, or the gods of the Amorites in whose land you are living. As for me and my family, we will worship the LORD" (Josh. 24:15).

Write in the margin the "Shechems," painful or joyful, God has used to remind you that He alone is Lord and is able to lead you and love you through life's trials.

After Joshua assembled the leaders at Shechem and reminded them of God's goodness to them in the past, he challenged them to faithfulness. Joshua provided four reasons the children of Israel should willingly and uncompromisingly surrender to God. Let's consider the first two today and look at the other two tomorrow.

1. REMEMBER THE CALL

Abram, later to be called friend of God (see Isa. 41:8) and listed as an honoree in the great hall of faith (see Heb. 11), was a descendant of idol worshipers (see Josh. 24:2). Only the call of God transformed him into the covenant-keeper.

Notice that Abraham's past didn't disqualify him from being called by God and used for His service. Likewise, your past—no matter how sinful—cannot remove you from the reach of God's calling. The same God who called an idol worshiper has also called you with a holy calling (1 Tim. 1:9). He calls us to spiritually die to our sins so we might live new lives in Him.

In Genesis 12:1, what three things did God call Abram

to leave? _____

To move into the calling the Lord has for us, we must willingly leave some things behind. Anything or anybody that receives more of my worship than God does is an idol, including television, books, the Internet, or even a relationship. Even necessary and good things such as food and sleep can become idols if they become more important than God. God will not share us with anything or anyone that takes our eyes off Him.

2. REMEMBER THE PROMISE

You can't depend on many things in this world. But you can always count on one true thing—God's Word. If the Father decrees it, then it will come to pass. In Joshua 24:3-4 God told the children of Israel to remember

His promise to Abraham. In doing so, God reminded the people of His faithfulness. Power resides in remembering God's promises.

Look up these passages and draw a line to match the reference below to the promise God makes to us.

Deuteronomy 31:6   **God equips us to do what He calls us to do.**

Romans 8:39   **God will never leave us.**

Isaiah 61:1-3   **Nothing can separate us from the love of God.**

day Four

Committed to Serve

Today, as we discuss the third and fourth reasons for choosing obedience, we will focus more intently on God's commitment to guide us. He is our protector and the source of our life-purpose. Understanding these important truths will better position us to hear His voice.

3. Remember the Protection

As a freshman at the University of Houston, I excitedly took three of my friends for a ride in my first car. The night was rainy, and as I stopped for a red light, my car began to skid. The resulting accident involved not only my car but three others. I ended up on the pavement, looking at headlights rushing at me, and thought, *My life is over*. But God had other plans. He protected me from that oncoming car.

Look up the verses on the next page in your Bible and note below what each says about God's protection.

Take Action

When we commit to a life of sanctification without compromise, we will inevitably hear God's voice more clearly. Pray this prayer:

"Heavenly Father, I will remember Your call on my life and Your promises. I commit to leave behind things that take my attention away from You. Like Abraham, I will follow you so that I might pursue your calling on my life. I desire to live a sanctified life—not out of guilt—but out of a grateful heart. God, thank You for all You've given me. Today, determined to die to the old and live uncompromisingly for You by the Holy Spirit's power, I start anew. In Jesus' name I pray, Amen."

Write today's date here

_____

Deuteronomy 23:14: _____

2 Samuel 22:31: _____

Psalm 46:1: _____

Psalm 62:7: _____

Our loving God is a refuge, a stronghold, a defender, and protector. God certainly doesn't protect us from hardship and trouble, but He protects us through them, even to heaven's door.

Stop and read Joshua 24:4-12. Notice that in every verse of this passage Joshua reminded them how God protects and brings to pass His own promises.

Take Action

For what good things do you tend to take credit when the credit belongs to the Father alone?

God is faithful to perform that which He has promised in spite of our sin, our complaints, and the roadblocks we put up.

How has God protected you in order to preserve His calling and promises? Plan to share your response with your group.

_____

4. REMEMBER THE SOURCE

Take time now to surrender those things back to God, giving Him all the credit.

Read Joshua 24:12-13. Who alone did Joshua remind the children of Israel was the source of their victory and the fulfillment of His promise? _____

After reminding the people of all God had done on their behalf, Joshua challenged the people to make a decision to be set apart to God without compromise: "Choose for yourselves today whom you will serve" (Josh. 24:15, NASB). Having a relationship with God that results in intimate communication begins with a decision. We must immediately and urgently decide to fear the Lord and serve Him in sincerity and truth.

Obedience from the Heart

What do 1 Samuel 15:22 and Jeremiah 7:23 state as a

true desire of God? _____

We have all done things "for God" out of religious duty instead of a sincere heart that is eager to obey the Father. In Romans 6:17, Paul stressed the core of lifestyle sanctification as a sincere heart passion to obey. Matthew 22:37 tells us to, "Love the Lord your God with all your heart, with all your soul, and with all your mind."

Think about the religious activities or good deeds you do. Sometimes we do things simply because they are the right thing to do or because we are following tradition. But if our hearts are not behind good deeds, we will miss the blessing and joy available to us through our service. Only actions built on our love for God and an honest desire to please Him will do.

When you face an unpleasant task, how would your attitude change if you saw it as your personal act of

worship? _____

_____

When we forget that our entire life is an act of worship, we can begin to take the short cut. After all, everyone's doing it. Let's live differently. Let's practice honoring God in the little things of life. The more nobody notices, the more we can enjoy the private affirmation of the Father. In the process we'll be positioning ourselves at His feet and listening for His voice.

[1]J.F. Walvoord and Roy B. Zuck, *The Bible Knowledge Commentary: An Exposition of the Scriptures* (Wheaton: Victor Books, 1998). electronic ed.

Daily Bread

"The Lord said: Because these people approach Me with their mouths to honor Me with lip service—yet their hearts are far from Me, and their worship consists of man-made rules learned by rote—therefore I will again confound these people with wonder after wonder. The wisdom of their wise men will vanish, and the understanding of the perceptive will be hidden" (Isa. 29:13-14).

Take Action

Complete these sentences with the actions you need to implement to be set apart like Samuel when He heard God speak.

I will seek to die daily to _____

not compromise in _____

serve from passion rather than tradition when _____

NOTES

Before the Session

For step 2, provide a marker and a writing surface divided into two columns. Label one *Worldly Freedom* and the other *Freedom in Christ*.

During the Session

1. Ask: *Why do parents warn their children, "Remember your last name,"* *as they walk out the door?* OR Ask: *What makes your family/home* *different from the other families/homes in your community? Is this differ-* *ence a choice or coincidence? Do you like being different or wish you could* *blend in a little more? Explain.* FOR EITHER OPTION: Declare that since God's children reflect Him, He desires that we be set apart from this world, not blend in.

2. Ask how we can know from 1 Samuel 3:1 that it was unusual for Samuel to hear God speak. Explain that Samuel was obviously set apart. Ask the class to identify the theological term for "set apart" [sanctified]. Request someone read aloud Romans 6:6-7. Lead the class to determine what sets believers apart. Allow volunteers to share the signs they listed for the first activity of Day 1 (p. 125). Guide learners to determine from 1 Corinthians 15:31-34 and 1 Peter 1:13-16 responsibilities of those who have been set apart. Call attention to the writing surface you prepared. Ask which freedom leads to blending in and which leads to being set apart. Guide the class to contrast the two freedoms. [Sample: sexual promiscuity versus true intimacy in marriage] Record responses.

3. Read the opening question of Day 2 (p. 127). Ask: *According to Romans* *6:5 and Philippians 3:10, what has God provided that's even better than* *superhero status?* [divine power] Declare: *We must be set apart* from *sin* *and death and set apart* to *life and godliness.* Discuss the first activity of Day 2. Ask how believers can possibly obey those commands. Request someone read aloud Ephesians 1:18-20. Ask what kind of power is at work within believers. [See the three headings in Day 2.] Discuss the challenges learners listed in the activity on the top of page 128. Ask: *How* *can believers activate this kind of power?* Read aloud Philippians 2:13 and lead the class to discuss the *Take Action* in the margin of page 129.

4. Ask: *Do you think a sanctified life is possible if we set our lives on "default mode"? Explain.* Explain that a set-apart life is established and maintained by a firm decision. Read aloud Joshua 24:15. Direct learners to determine from Joshua 24:1 where this commitment ceremony occurred. Ask: *What does Mrs. Shirer say are our Shechems? Why would God take us back there to prepare us to hear Him speak?* Allow volunteers to share their responses to the first activity of Day 3 (p. 130).

5. Explain that four reasons God's people should willingly be set apart for God can be found in Joshua 24. Request someone read aloud Joshua 24:2. Invite someone to read aloud Genesis 12:1-3. Ask: *What did God call Abram to? What did He call him from? What must we leave behind to move into God's call?* Urge learners that if they want to hear God speak, they must remember His call and His promise. Find in Joshua 24:3-4 God's fulfilled promises to Abraham. Complete the final activity of Day 3 (p. 131). Explore how remembering God's promises helps believers hear God speak.

6. State: *We must also remember God's protection.* Guide the class to find in Joshua 24:4-12 how God protected His people. Discuss the Scriptures from the first activity of Day 4 (pp. 131-132). Allow learners to give examples of God's protection from the activity in the middle of page 132. Comment that there was one more thing of which God's people needed to be reminded as an incentive to serve God alone. Complete the final activity in Day 4 to discover the answer. Discuss the *Take Action* question on page 132 in general rather than personal terms. Ask: *How will understanding that God is our protector and the source of our power and life-purpose better position us to hear His voice?*

7. Assert: *When we remember God's call, promise, protection, and provision, there's still something else we must do if we're to be set apart to hear when He speaks. What is that according to Joshua 24:14-15?* Point out that our choice to worship God alone should be out of love for Him, not out of religious duty. Discuss the first activity of Day 5 (p. 133). Discover in Isaiah 29:13; Matthew 22:37; and Romans 6:17 the kind of obedience God desires. Lead adults to contrast ritual obedience with from-the-heart obedience. Discuss the second activity of Day 5 and examine how this would set learners apart so, like Samuel, they can hear from God in a time when others aren't hearing. Request learners silently consider the *Take Action* in the margin of Day 5. Close in prayer.

A Still Attentiveness

day One

Still in My Mind

Our minds are battlefields, not theme parks! Two forces are "raised up" against our ability to clearly hear God's voice. This truth becomes apparent when we can't sleep, eat, or think straight because of the tug-of-war within our heads. Our frantic attempts to fix our own problems keep us from hearing God's calming voice, receiving His instructions.

Look closely at 2 Corinthians 10:5, found in the margin. Underline the two forces that oppose the knowledge of God.

"Samuel was lying down *in the temple of the LORD where the ark of God was"* (1 Sam. 3:3, NASB).

Samuel was still.

From lustful thoughts to regretful ones, guilty reminders of the past to vengeful imaginations, our minds fill with images that can pull us away from the Lord, His voice, and His plan for our lives. Today we'll look at a strategy for winning the spiritual war for our minds.

We must consider three questions as we prepare to fight this battle. Who is our enemy? What are our weapons? What is our battle strategy?

The True Enemy

Daily Bread

"We are destroying speculations and every lofty thing raised up against the knowledge of God, and we are taking every thought captive to the obedience of Christ" (2 Cor.10:5, NASB)

According to 1 Peter 5:8 who is our adversary? _____

Fighting tirelessly against negative thoughts is futile since they are not our real enemy. Instead, we must concern ourselves with the true enemy of our souls. When we listen to God's voice, the Devil fears us. So he will do anything to hinder us from hearing from God. He actively roams the earth seeking whom he may destroy (see Job 2:2), and he wants to use our minds as tools to destroy us.

When I recognize the enemy as I struggle with lustful, fearful, or guilty thoughts, I get angry! That righteous anger energizes me. God intends for us to get mad when the Devil infiltrates our thoughts. When we recognize our true enemy we know where to direct our spiritual weaponry.

The Weapons

Satan's goal and desire is to fill our minds with arguments and strongholds that will keep us from a close relationship with God.

Check the examples of satanic argument, found in the margin, that he has used on you lately.

Paul understood that his business was to "demolish arguments and every high-minded thing that is raised up against the knowledge of God" (2 Cor. 10:3-5). Paul realized human wisdom would not tear down the barriers and strongholds in the minds of the people to whom he preached. He also knew these would keep people from hearing God's voice.

The Battle Strategy

I know a woman who struggled with an eating disorder for more than a decade. Satan used her mind to keep her in bondage by continually filling it with destructive thoughts. I asked how she won the war of her mind. She told me she purposely filled her mind with the Word of God. When the Holy Spirit supernaturally applies the Word of God to your life, you can begin to gain control over your thought life. To know and understand the Scriptures is to know and understand God's power (see Mark 12:24).

Think of the Scripture as your "dagger." Every time you feel your mind running away with inappropriate thoughts or imaginations, quickly jab those thoughts with the Word.

Search the following passages to learn how to respond to some specific negative thoughts.
Fill in the chart with your findings.

❑ Disobedience doesn't really have serious consequences (see Gen. 3:4).

❑ You can do better as your own boss (see Gen. 3:5).

❑ You should be free to worship as you choose (see Matt. 4:8-10).

❑ You aren't valuable to God or anyone else (see Matt. 10:30-31).

❑ Your sins are too numerous for God to forgive (see Isa. 44:21-22).

Negative Thought	Scripture Reference	Truth
I am inadequate.	1 Peter 1:3	

I've messed up too much in my past.	**Philippians 3:13**
I'll never be free from this sin.	**John 8:36**
I'm insignificant.	**Jeremiah 1:5**
I'm a mistake.	**Psalm 139:14**

In the margin on page 137, briefly describe one negative thought with which you struggle. Search Scripture to find a "dagger" to use against that thought. Consider using a concordance, a topical Bible, or Bible software.

day Two

Still in My Confidence

The very foundation of Christianity is our faith in Christ's ability to forgive our sins through the sacrifice of His life and the victory of His resurrection. Today we will look at the concept of confidence, exploring its role in our ongoing relationship with Christ.

Read Ruth 1:5-22. According to the last line of verse 16, in whom did Ruth place her confidence?_____

Ruth trusted Naomi, but she ultimately placed her trust in Naomi's God. Ruth set an example for us to follow. In Ruth 3 Boaz, Ruth's employer, commended her not only for her initial confidence in God but also for her ongoing faith despite her circumstances.

Read in Ruth 2:11-12 the circumstances that Boaz mentions that could have caused Ruth's confidence in God

to waver. **What circumstances in your life cause your faith to waver?**

_____

Have you sought refuge in God for those situations?
❏ **Yes**   ❏ **No**

How? _____

Just as salvation can only come when we truly transfer our confidence from ourselves to Jesus, our ability to live victorious Christian lives comes only as we place that same confidence in Christ daily. Whether in business or personal matters we usually find assurance when we are self-reliant. It's so easy for us to trust in ourselves, but it is difficult for most of us to admit our faults, face our weakness, and ask God for the help we need.

In Luke 5:31 Jesus clearly stated that He came for those who are sick and in need of help. Jesus likened Himself to a physician. Like any good doctor, He's available to people who are aware they are sick, admit they are sick, and come to Him with confidence.

Read 1 Timothy 1:15-16, printed in the margin, and answer the following: What did Jesus come to do?

_____

What did Paul admit about himself?

_____

What did Paul find as a result of this?

_____

God can turn our circumstances around when we admit our needs and place our confidence in Him alone.

Daily Bread

"Jesus replied, 'The healthy don't need a doctor, but the sick do'" (Luke 5:31).

"This saying is trustworthy and deserving of full acceptance: 'Christ Jesus came into the world to save sinners'—and I am the worst of them. But I received mercy because of this, so that in me, the worst of them, Christ Jesus might demonstrate the utmost patience as an example to those who would believe in Him for eternal life" (1 Tim. 1:15-16).

After admitting our need to the doctor and placing confidence in him, we must daily follow the doctor's recipe for recovery. The confidence we have in the doctor's ability shows up in how faithfully we stick to the physician's instructions.

In Luke 5 Jesus sat with tax collectors and sinners, people ostracized by the community. The banquet was in the home of a tax collector named Levi who would later be called Matthew. In response to Jesus' command to follow Him, Levi invited Jesus into his home for a celebration and reception.

Jesus' "prescription" to Levi in Luke 5:27 is the same as His instruction to us.

Write it. _____

Levi left behind his family, career, money, friends, home, security, and much more because he believed Christ had more to offer. So confident was he in this decision that he threw a party to celebrate!

Why would a man find cause for celebration in "leaving everything behind" (v. 28)?

_____

I think the account points to a basic misconception. We don't really give up anything to follow Christ. Instead, we make a wise value judgment. Levi believed the man for whom he left everything was more valuable than what he gave up.

day Three

Still in My Emotions

Not only had Ruth lost her husband, but she also had relocated to a new place where she likely did not know the language or the social customs. Her life was not easy. Such hardships and difficulties could have emotionally destroyed her. Ruth must have been somewhat like my friend Jenny. Read Jenny's story printed in the margin.

Tough circumstances can easily get the best of us emotionally. Yet Scripture shows Ruth dealing with her circumstances extremely well. She expressed her emotions (see Ruth 1:9,14), but we don't see her overcome by them. How did Old Testament Ruth and modern America Jenny rest so assuredly in the arms of God while in such personal pain?

What hardship are you facing right now in your life?

_____

Runaway Feelings

You are certainly not alone if hard times make you weep or grow angry. Emotions are not wrong. In fact, God Himself exhibits many emotions ranging from joy (see Zeph. 3:17) to anger (see 2 Kings 21:6). We know that Jesus was sinless (see 2 Cor. 5:21), but even He experienced anger (see Mark 3:5) and a sadness that caused Him to weep (see John 11:35). The problem is that many of us allow our feelings to dictate our actions, affect our decisions, or worse, justify inappropriate actions. Runaway emotions can block God's voice and keep us from following God's plan for our lives. Feelings should never be the final decision-maker in our lives.

What emotions do you struggle to keep under control?

_____

Emotions do serve us in another way—they provide a window into our minds and hearts. They reveal what we believe.

When Jackson was three months old, we moved him from the bassinet in our room to his upstairs nursery. My imagination created potential scenarios in which my baby was somehow hurt. Fear consumed me. Finally remembering that God is always in full control, I had a decision to make. Would I allow fear to control my actions by stealing my sleep or even causing me to sleep in my child's room? Or would I let go of my fears,

Jenny has every right to be an emotional basket case, but her smile shows the security and peace she finds in the Lord. Nothing in Jenny's life seems easy. She has had 50 operations to try to cure a muscular disease that puzzles her doctors. She has never known a day without extreme pain. Jenny's father was killed by a doctor's error. Her mother will have eight operations over the next few years to deal with her own medical problems. Despite all of this Jenny says, "I thank God for every single thing I have lived through."

"Be angry and do not sin. Don't let the sun go down on your anger, and don't give the Devil an opportunity" (Eph. 4:26-27).

Take Action

Instead of allowing your emotions to steer you away from God, purposefully turn your attention to the Lord in times of intense emotional stress. Be honest about your struggles and ask Him to reveal His perspective and power. Talk to the Lord about any emotions you are experiencing. Ask Him to help you be emotionally still so your actions can be controlled by what you know to be true rather than by what you feel.

Write your prayer:

giving them to God? My display of fear exposed to me the gap between what I said I believed and what I really felt.

Banking on God's Promises

Ephesians 4:26-27 (see the margin) clearly warns that allowing our emotions to gain control of our actions gives Satan an avenue and opportunity to work in our lives. Remembering God's promises helps us greatly in the task of controlling our emotions.

Read the following verses. Summarize the encouragements God gave to these individuals.

Genesis 15:1 _____

Deuteronomy 31:6_____

1 Chronicles 28:20 _____

Isaiah 41:13 _____

Are you lonely? The Lord says, "I am with you always" (Matt. 28:20). Are you afraid? The Lord says, "My peace I give to you" (John 14:27). Are you anxious or worried? The Lord says, "Though the mountains move and the hills shake, My love will not be removed from you" (Isa. 54:10). Are you angry and seeking revenge? The Lord says, "Vengeance is mine. I will repay" (Rom. 12:19).

Experiencing emotion is not wrong; letting emotions consume and control us is. Let God's promises show you how to think and act.

day Four

Still in My Ambitions

Before I understood God's calling on my life, I wanted to be a Christian singer. Door after door closed in my face. Yet instead of accepting that

God wanted me to move in a different direction, I allowed my ambition to turn into selfishness. I began to disregard God's leading, trying to kick the doors of the music industry down on my own. All that time I spent trying so hard to make things happen, I was fighting against God's will. Too often we don't hear the voice of God because we fear God might ask us to do something that goes against our plans.

Describe a time when you could not turn loose of your desires.

_____

Which of the following best describes your ambitions?

❑ **make more money** ❑ **have children**

❑ **get married** ❑ **keep a youthful appearance**

❑ **start a ministry** ❑ **get a degree**

❑ **get promoted** ❑ **take a dream vacation**

Problems with Ambition

Ambition implies a desire and willingness to do whatever it takes to reach a goal. Ambitious people are in danger of being controlled by ambition rather than the voice of God.

Our ambitions often reveal a deeper desire for status, fame, or power. Most of what we strive for and desire finds its root in one of those three areas. Paul called these desires "confidence in the flesh" (Phil. 3:3-4). Worldly ambition is a desire to find fulfillment in the things that please us instead of pleasing God.

Describe how the following Scriptures speak to the issue of our ambition.

Ecclesiastes 2:11 _____

Matthew 6:26-34 _____

John 14:27 _____

Daily Bread

"Be still, and know that I am God: I will be exalted among the nations, I will be exalted in the earth" (Ps. 46:10, ASV).

Take Action

Proverbs 16:3 applauds people who plan wisely to reach their goals. Ultimately, we must relax in the knowledge that God is sovereign and His design for our lives is better than our own. Ambition must not control our actions.

• *How might ambition hurt your ability to hear from God?*

• *Have you crossed the line from godly planning to selfish ambition in some area of your life?*

• *Tell God that you desire His plans more than your own and that you are willing to exchange your selfish ambition for His agenda for your life.*

Still in My Actions

Daily Bread

"Your strength will come from settling down in complete dependence on me" (Isa. 30:15, The Message).

Life seems to press in on my quiet time, pulling my attention away from God. Sometimes it seems so hard to find the time to sit still before Him. Yet the simple instruction to "be still" permeates Scripture. In Isaiah 30 God spoke to obstinate Israelites determined to go about their plans without regard for His.

Take Action

How can you alter your schedule to make time to be still before God? List practical steps you will take to prioritize listening for God's voice.

What was Israel trying to do that was not pleasing to God (Isa. 30:1-2)?

_____

• *To have a daily quiet time, I will*

The Israelites did everything in their power to try to solve the problem. Unfortunately, nothing seemed to work. In the midst of all of their efforts God said, "In quietness and rest is your strength." God may be calling us to be still in Him instead of trying to work things out on our own.

• *To remind myself to pray throughout the day I will*

Their history could have taught the Israelites what to do in their time of need. Instead of frantically seeking his own solution when an enemy army was approaching, King Jehoshaphat simply looked to God.

Read 2 Chronicles 20:6-17. Paraphrase God's response to Jehoshaphat's prayer in verse 17.

• *To quiet myself when worries overtake me I will*

_____

The decision to consciously submit to repentance, rest, quiet, and trust is a conscious commitment that requires courage, effort, and diligence. Our job in the battle is to station ourselves. Sometimes the most difficult response you can make to a challenge is to sit quietly before the Lord.

• *To practice trusting the Father more I will*

[1] *"Papers of Philip James Elliot—Collection 277,"* Billy Graham Center archives [online], [cited 19 January 2005]. *Available from the Internet http://www.wheaton.edu/bgc/archives/faq/20.htm.*

leader Guide

Before the Session

Provide 2 Corinthians 10:5 in several versions of the Bible as suggested in Step 2.

During the Session

1. Read aloud Psalm 46:10. Lead the class to explore the relationship between being still, knowing God, and hearing God speak. OR Request learners indicate whether they would have been described as a calm or hyper child and estimate how many times they were told to "be still" when they were growing up. Ask for reasons parents admonish their children to "be still." FOR EITHER OPTION: Direct learners to find in 1 Samuel 3:3-4 what Samuel was doing when God spoke to him. Declare: *God spoke to Samuel not when he was rushing but resting. He also tells us to be still so we can hear Him when He speaks.*

2. Determine whether it is easier to be mentally or physically still and why. Discuss the first activity of Day 1 (p. 136). Explore specific speculations and lofty things that strive to pull our minds away from God. [It might help to read this verse in several contemporary versions that can be found on *www.biblegateway.com.*] Encourage learners that it is possible for us to experience victory in this war for our minds. Ask why it is imperative to know your enemy if you're going to win a battle. Discuss the second activity of Day 1. Consider how viewing Satan, rather than our thoughts, as the real enemy gives us a new perspective in the battle. Ask: *What kind of weapons does Satan use to keep believers from a close relationship with God?* Encourage them to add other lies Satan tells people to the list in the margin. Request someone read aloud 2 Corinthians 10:3-5. Ask: *What kind of weapons must we use to fight our spiritual enemy? What is our main weapon? What is the battle strategy for using that weapon?* Call attention to the *Take Action* in the margin of page 138. List Paul's suggestions. Complete the final activity of Day 1 [begins on p. 137]. Challenge the class to state true, noble, or lovely thoughts that would combat the negative thoughts listed in the chart.

To the Leader:

Purposefully practice being still this week. Get away from all distractions, meditate on Psalm 46 or Isaiah 30:1-26, and listen to God when He speaks to you. Be prepared to share your own experience in stillness as the class discusses each day's lessons on "A Still Attentiveness."

3. Request someone read aloud Luke 5:31. Ask: *Are you quick or slow to go to the doctor? Why? Who are the people doctors can help?* Declare that Jesus, like any doctor, can only help people who acknowledge they need healing. Organize the class into three groups. Request Group One read 2 Chronicles 20:1-4,22 and note how the persons admitted their need for God and what happened as a result. Group Two is to do the same with Mark 10:46-52, and Group Three with Luke 8:43-48. Allow groups to share. Ask learners how they demonstrate confidence in their doctor. Discuss the Day 2 activity regarding Jesus' "prescription" (p. 140). Discuss the *Take Action* questions in the margin and then the final activity of Day 2. Explore how obeying Jesus' prescription will lead believers to be still in their confidence.

4. Request learners identify Ruth's difficult circumstances from Ruth 2:11 and her accompanying emotions in 1:9,14. Ask: *Are the emotions we have about our trials wrong? When do emotions become a problem?* Request someone read aloud Ephesians 4:26-27. Read aloud the Scriptures listed in the final activity of Day 3 (p. 142) and determine how each divine promise can help believers still any emotions that threaten to overtake them. Admonish learners that quieting our emotions does not happen by default but by purposefully surrendering to God in times of stress.

5. Ask: *Would you classify ambition as a positive or negative attribute? Why?* Request the same three groups from Step 3 read one of the following passages and identify the ambition and God's response: Genesis 3:5-6,14-19; Genesis 11:1-9; Isaiah 14:12-15. Urge learners to silently consider the questions in the *Take Action* in the margin of page 143. Read aloud Proverbs 16:1-9. Guide the class to pull out of this passage principles that can help believers learn to be still in their ambitions so they please God and put themselves in a position to hear God when He speaks.

6. Ask learners if they think there are times when we need to be physically still before God and why. Discuss the first activity of Day 5 (p. 144). Request learners state from Isaiah 30:15 what God urged the Israelites to do and how they responded. Read aloud the final paragraph of Day 5. Guide the class to determine why the concluding statement is true. Work together to list practical steps under the *Take Action* in the margin on page 144. Close in prayer that God will empower each learner to be still and hear Him speak.

A Sold-Out Hunger

day One

Hungry for His Direction

In Exodus 33:12-13 we find Moses hungry for clear guidance from the Lord. He prayed earnestly for clarification of the directions God had given him. He wanted to follow *God's* plan and purposes instead of his own.

Which of the following best describes how you seek God's direction?
- ❏ **I desire to understand His purposes for me.**
- ❏ **I seek God's blessing on my plans.**
- ❏ **Sometimes I follow Him; sometimes I follow me.**

Your Interruption: God's Intervention

Each day I ask the Lord to guide me. Unfortunately, however, I often become frustrated when God changes my plans to coincide with His. In truth, we all become frustrated when seemingly meaningless interruptions interfere with plans for our careers, families, finances, or ministries. Are we missing God's intervention as He diverts us to His will?

What does Isaiah 55:8-9 reveal about the differences between our plans and the Lord's?

_____

God sees the big picture. He's in control.

Think of a time when God redirected your plans to His. How did you respond? Plan to share your story.

_____

DIGITAL VIDEO 🖥️

If you would be interested in watching Priscilla Shirer herself discuss the material in this *MasterWork* lesson—and more— go to *www.lifeway.com* and purchase your personal copy of the digital video for Session 5 of *He Speaks to Me*.

"Samuel was lying down in the temple of the LORD where the ark of God was" *(1 Sam. 3:3, NASB).*

Samuel got as close as he could to the manifest presence of God.

Daily Bread

"He, your Teacher will no longer hide Himself, but your eyes will behold your Teacher. Your ears will hear a word behind you, 'This is the way, walk in it, whenever you turn to the right or to the left'" (Isa. 30:20-21, NASB).

147

Can you commit to trusting in God's direction even when it seems contrary to what you think you need?

Describe an occasion when you executed a plan that was not from God.

What indicators or interruptions were placed in your path to show you that your plans weren't His?

List areas of your life where you need to fervently and completely seek God's guidance.

Before I met my husband, my plans for becoming a wife were repeatedly "interrupted," leaving me frustrated and emotional. When I met Jerry and we cautiously approached the idea of marriage together, I was timid and afraid. Hoping for answers, I prayed, searched Scripture, and sought the wise counsel of the minister who had officiated my parents' wedding ceremony. He said something that changed my perspective: "Priscilla, if God used those interruptions to guide you to His will, He can and will interrupt anything that goes against His plans for you now. Your job is to be hungry enough to receive His direction. He will reveal it to you." What a freeing thought for me! Relieved, I rejoiced in the life interruptions that had led me to Jerry and found renewed trust in God's guidance.

Think about the Israelites, trudging across the desert, grumbling and complaining as they traveled. They brought immense suffering on their heads because they trusted their own wisdom instead of God's. Like the Jews, we are often willing to experience hardship simply because we want to follow our own direction instead of consulting God.

Read Isaiah 30:8-21. According to verse 18, what is the Lord waiting to show his people?

_____

What does He tell those who wait for His guidance

(v. 21)? _____

day *Two*

Hungry for His Word

As we seek God's direction and listen for His reply, we must wisely verify that the voice of response is God's and not our own. But how can we make sure that our own voice—our desires and wants—isn't drowning out God's? Before we can answer that, we have to address the fact that everyone seems to claim, "I've heard from God." A man insists God told him to leave his wife and children. Supposedly the same God who spoke to Moses instructs physicians to end the lives of unborn children and elderly adults. Obviously, God did not really say those things.

We must learn to reconcile what people claim to "hear" God say with the truth of what God really says. Just as important, we must investigate how we can apply that knowledge to our relationship with the Lord.

The Bible Is Our Standard

When Moses wanted to know the way of the Lord, He went to God directly and asked for His word. You want to know God? You want to discern His voice from your own? Get to know His written Word. Scripture touches on every aspect of our lives, from finances to family matters.

God's spoken word can always be backed up by His written Word. Individuals who "hear from God" without taking time to verify the message against Scripture risk falling into grave error.

Even the most well-intentioned individuals who desire to obey God can misunderstand His instructions. The confusion and chaos of work, family, finances, sin, and even traditionalism can prevent us from clearly hearing God's voice. Scripture descrambles the distortion by either authenticating or disproving what we think we have heard.

In the margin make note of "environmental elements" in your life right now that might affect your ability to clearly hear God's voice.

The Bible Is Absolute Truth

God will *never* give us fresh spoken words that contradict His written Word. The Bible alone provides the foundational directives you and I need to make decisions that glorify God. Apart from reliance on the truth of Scripture, we cannot clearly hear Him.

According to 2 Timothy 3:16-17, found in the margin, how much of Scripture is inspired by God? _____

Think about a major decision you might make. Which of the following honestly expresses your biggest concern?

Daily Bread

"All Scripture is inspired by God and is profitable for teaching, for rebuking, for correcting, for training in righteousness, so that the man of God may be complete, equipped for every good work" (2 Tim. 3:16-17).

"Every part of Scripture is God-breathed and useful one way or another—showing us truth, exposing our rebellion, correcting our mistakes, training us to live God's way. Through the Word we are put together and shaped up for the tasks God has for us" (2 Tim. 3:16-17, The Message).

Take Action

If an observer were to evaluate your current decision-making process, what would it reveal about whether or not you truly know the Lord?

Think about a time when you obeyed God in a difficult situation.

• *How did Scripture's truth change your decision?*

• *How did your obedience result in deeper intimacy with Him?*

Renew your commitment to God's Word. Lay your hand on the Bible and tell the Lord that you will trust His words as the ultimate basis for all your decisions regardless of the way you feel.

❏ **I worry what my people might say about my choice.**
❏ **I want the option that is the most convenient.**
❏ **I wonder which decision might prove the most personally profitable.**
❏ **I'm curious to know what Scripture says about this.**

I must always adjust my personal decisions to line up with Scripture. The more I learn about the Bible, the better I become at this. We must not only recognize Scripture as God's truth, we must also obey it.

Read Proverbs 3:5-6. What does it means to "not rely on your own understanding"?

_____

When we devote ourselves to reading Scripture, it becomes a part of us, reminding us of its precepts and encouraging us to obey its guidelines. For instance, a recent family situation bothered me for some time. I found myself complaining about it constantly, but the Holy Spirit convicted me about my negative attitude through two important Scriptures. James 5:9 says, "Do not complain about one another, so that you will not be judged." First Peter 4:9 says that we should "be hospitable to one another without complaining." Though Scripture's message to me was clear, I didn't immediately stop complaining—at least not until I came across 1 John 2:3-6.

Read 1 John 2:3-6. What is the determining factor that reveals whether or not someone truly knows the Lord?

_____

The term "know" as used in verse 4 of 1 John 2 is the Greek word *ginosko*, meaning "to know intimately"—not to just have a casual relationship but to know details about someone in a way that is special and specific to only the two of you. The closer you get to God, the more frequently and readily you will hear and identify the voice of God speaking to you. Intimacy and closeness with Him should be our continuous desire.

day Three

Hungry for His Presence

What stunning comment did God make in Exodus 33:3-4 that caused the people to mourn?

_____

_____

Daily Bread

"Moses had one more request. 'Please let me see your glorious presence' "
(Ex. 33:18, NLT).

God told Moses to continue his journey into the promised land, but can you imagine Moses' distress as God said He would withdraw from the Israelites? God had faithfully delivered him in the most dramatic fashion we could imagine. Yet Moses needed more than God's victory over his enemies or power to lead the people, more than physical food and water, and more than another miracle. He wanted to experience the overwhelming presence of the Lord—nothing less would satisfy.

"Please," Moses asked, *desperate* for divine guidance and direction in Exodus 33:18, "let me see your glorious presence!" As I imagine the scene, I can almost hear Moses pleading: "Don't give up on us, Lord! I need You. I trust You. Guide me! Meet with me! Lead me!"

God desires followers desperate for His presence—people who don't necessarily want His blessings but want Him! God wants followers like Moses, who balk at the idea of going anywhere without His leading. Not only is His presence the only means of salvation, but it is also the only distinguishing characteristic between the followers of God and those who follow different gods (Ex. 33:16). We need to experience His *manifest* presence.

Omnipresence =
God's ability to be present in all places at all times.

The following words describe the term *manifest*: *obvious, clear, visible, marked, noticeable, observable.* In the margin, write how God's manifest presence is different from His omnipresence.

Why God Removes His Manifest Presence

God knows that His people will sin, but He refuses to bless a place where people are stubborn, rebellious, and set in their own ways (see Ex. 33:5). God becomes especially angered with those who arrogantly continue in their sin when confronted.

Read Deuteronomy 9:6-12. How long had the Israelites been obstinate (v. 7)? _____

When the people became impatient waiting for Moses, what did they fill their time doing (vv. 9-12)?

_____

Are you living an obstinate lifestyle before God in any area of your life right now? If so, how?

_____

A Matter of the Heart

Stubbornness quenches our thirst for God. If we are not seeing the presence of God in our lives, it may be because we lack a hunger and thirst for Him. If you find you do not pant for Him as the deer pants for water (see Ps. 42:1), evaluate yourself to see if you have become stiff-necked and ask the Lord to restore your passion. God promises He will meet with those who hunger and thirst for Him (see Isa. 41:17).

day *Four*

Hungry for His Peace

Recently my husband and I were at odds about a particular situation. Every time I decided to bring up the issue I felt the Ruler of my heart throw up a warning flag, yet ahead I went. I spoke in a peaceful tone, but I

Take Action

Ask the Lord to forgive any rebellion that keeps you from desperately seeking Him and experiencing His manifest presence.

Read Matthew 5:6. Ask Him to give you a genuine thirst for Him as you seek to follow His plan for your life. Trust in the promise of His Word.

Daily Bread

"The peace of God, which surpasses every thought, will guard your hearts and your minds in Christ Jesus" (Phil. 4:7).

was blatantly ignoring the lack of peace in my heart. As a result, my peace and my marriage both suffered.

Read Colossians 3:15, printed in the margin. Circle the quality that should rule in our hearts.

"Let the peace of Christ rule in your hearts, to which indeed you were called in one body; and be thankful" (Col. 3:15, NASB).

Peace Rules

As Christians, we have built-in meters to gauge our behavior. The Holy Spirit works in us, urging us to check our actions against what we know is right. When we get off track, we may experience guilt or even suffer consequences. But when our lives align with God's plans, we find peace.

In Exodus 33:13-15 Moses requested, "Lord, teach me your ways." Then he said, "Please, Lord, don't make us go without You." Each time I read Exodus, I am touched by God's comforting response to Moses' pleas: "My presence will go with you. I will give you rest." Peace results from God's presence in our lives. Peace brings rest, tranquility, assuredness, security, and safety. When we experience the lack of quiet rest, we need to ask if our hearts may be sensing the absence of God's presence or approval.

Our Relationship with Peace

So what must we do to have God's peace? We need never to take lightly those decisions or plans that leave our hearts in turmoil. When you feel a tug of war ensuing in your heart, pay close attention. Peace or a lack of it can settle a debate or argument for us, leading to correct decisions.

Let me issue a warning. We can ignore the voice of God and go on quite comfortably it seems. A carnal or backslidden Christian can experience the false peace of a dull conscience.

Signs of False Peace

The Bible gives us several practical ways to discern God's will and distinguish between true and false peace. These red flags can help us determine if we are outside God's will even when we sleep soundly at night.

Red Flag #1: Are we running away? Consider Jonah's story.

Read Jonah 1:1-3. Write in the margin what Jonah was trying to do after receiving God's instructions.

153

Paraphrase what Psalm 139:7-10 suggests about the foolishness of Jonah's logic.

_____

_____

No matter where we go—God is there. No matter how we rebel, He is still in charge. Jonah learned that lesson the hard way.

Red Flag #2: Are we compensating? We can tell something is wrong internally when we try to fill the void with external things in an effort to escape the lack of peace inside. But real peace comes from within. It will not come until we repent before the Lord, seek His will, and begin to walk in it.

Red Flag #3: Are we thankful? Colossians 3:15 not only talks about peace but tells us to "be thankful." The Spirit can give you thankfulness for the surprising ways He helps you cope despite your circumstances. When peace rules in your heart, thankfulness and praise will be on your lips.

day Five

Hungry for His Power

As Moses negotiated with God, he said other nations would recognize the uniqueness of God's people because of the Lord's presence (see Ex. 33:16). For the Israelites, victory was secure as long as the presence of God was near. They understood that God's presence equals God's power. To draw near to God in the ways we have discussed throughout this study, we must have God's power.

God manifests His awesome presence to us through the power of the Holy Spirit. If you have accepted Christ, you have the Holy Spirit. He is a gift. The Holy Spirit's residence in our lives makes it possible for us to walk as victorious Christians. Though we can't physically see the Spirit, the effects of His presence are visible.

Match the following passages to the description of the Spirit's work.

___ empowers us to live godly lives   **a. John 16:13**

___ convicts us of our sin   **b. John 14:26**

___ teaches us what Jesus said   **c. 2 Peter 1:3**

___ guides us into all truth   **d. John 16:8**

Through the Holy Spirit we can exhibit love, joy, peace, patience, kindness, faithfulness, gentleness, goodness, and self control—even in those situations that make us want to rage or cry (see Gal. 5:22-23).

What task do you feel incapable of completing in your own power? _____

How might you handle the situation under the Spirit's influence? _____

Filled Full

God's Spirit lives in us (see 1 Cor. 3:16; 6:19). When we are "filled up" or controlled by the presence and power of the Holy Spirit, it will show in our actions. Being "filled with all the fullness of God" (Eph. 3:19) is a work God does for us. We must depend on Him. Our part is to be hungry for His power. Hungry people do whatever is necessary to be filled. When we show God spiritual hunger, He responds.

Really Changed

We ought to see a change when we're filled with the Spirit and under the influence of His power. Ephesians 5:18 contrasts being filled with the Spirit with being drunk with wine. When people are "drunk with wine," they do things they would not normally do. Paul mentioned some pretty major changes for most of us. I know I wouldn't naturally act in those ways apart from the power of the Spirit.

Read Ephesians 5:19-21. In the margin list the changes Paul said being filled with the Spirit makes.

Take Action

This week we've looked at hunger. It's easy to be hungry for food, but I want to hunger for Christ. I want to hunger for His direction, His presence, His peace, and His power.

Close out the week by asking God to make you hungry and thirsty for Him. Write your prayer below.

To the Leader:

Examine your meeting space with the eyes of a visitor. Is it cluttered? What's on the walls? Are there enough chairs so all learners feel there is a place for them, but not too many empty chairs so the room feels bare of people? Spend some time this week making your meeting space a welcoming and learning-conducive environment.

Before the Session

Set up a table with refreshments, such as doughnuts, muffins, coffee-cake, and coffee. [Step 1 Option]

During the Session

1. Ask: *When was the last time you were really hungry? Describe the actions and demeanor of a really hungry person.* OR As learners arrive, invite them to enjoy refreshments. Once your session begins, ask if learners were hungry when they came to Bible study today, and if so, what they did when they entered the room. Ask: *What one word best describes you when you get to the "I'm starving" stage?* FOR EITHER OPTION: Ask learners what they most want to eat when they're really hungry. Read aloud 1 Samuel 3:3. Remark that Samuel got as close as he could to the presence of God. Declare that if we want to hear God speak, we must be desperately hungry for Him.

2. Lead the class to identify what Moses was hungry for in Exodus 33:12-13. Ask: *Why might we lose our appetite for God's direction?* Declare that if we're going to ask for God's ways, we need to determine we're going to follow them. That means we need to see our interruptions as God's interventions. Discuss the second and third activities in Day 1 (p. 147). Explain that God's job is to guide us; our job is to be hungry enough to receive His direction. Complete the final activity of Day 1 (p. 148).

3. Consider what might affect our ability to clearly hear God's voice telling us the way to go. Ask Priscilla's question from the beginning of Day 2: *As we seek God's direction, how can we make sure our voice isn't drowning out God's?* State that if we want to hear God speak we must be desperately hungry for His Word. Request someone read aloud 2 Timothy 3:16-17. Inquire: *Why should we be hungry for this Word? How do we demonstrate that hunger? What must we do with God's Word besides read and study it? According to John 14:21, to whom will God reveal His ways and purposes? How does that truth make you even more hungry for His Word?*

4. Ask the question in the first activity of Day 3 (p. 151). Request a volunteer read aloud Exodus 33:1-2,15-16. Ask what God had promised to provide for the people and why that wasn't enough for them. Invite volunteers to share a time when they were so hungry for God's presence that an angel or promised blessing or protection simply would not do. Instruct learners to find in Exodus 33:17-18 what God promised and Moses' subsequent request. Ask what hunger Moses indicated by his request. Read aloud the third paragraph on page 151 (beginning with "God desires followers desperate for …"). Discuss the second activity on page 151. Read aloud Exodus 33:3,5 and ask why God removed His presence from His people in the first place. (Can any parents of toddlers or teens relate?!) Say: *Describe a stiff-necked person. Doesn't such a person desire God's presence? What will it take for us to "unstiffen" our necks and get hungry for God?*

5. Direct learners to find God's comforting response to Moses' pleas in Exodus 33:14. Ask if we always experience God's peace and why. Caution that if we ignore the Spirit's voice for too long, we can be lulled into a false peace. State from Day 4 the first and second red flags that discern if we are deluding ourselves into a false peace (pp. 153-154). Determine how believers can know if they are running away or compensating. Identify the third red flag. Request someone read aloud Colossians 3:15. Explore the connection between "being thankful" and "experiencing God's peace." Read the first paragraph of the *Take Action* in the margin of page 154. Evaluate how we can tell when we have or lack God's peace.

6. Guide the class to compare a power hungry person with a person who is hungry for God's power. Complete the first activity of Day 5 (p. 155). Ask: *With what does Ephesians 5:18 contrast being filled with the Spirit? How does alcohol change a person's behavior or personality? What fears and inhibitions can be overcome when we are filled with the Spirit?* Declare that believers must be so hungry for God's power that they surrender their lives to be filled with His Spirit.

7. Read aloud Matthew 5:6. Declare that God promises that if we hunger for Him, He'll fill us with Him, and we can hear Him speak. Close in prayer, asking God that participants will hunger for God.

A Servant Spirit

day One

Submissive to the Lord's Assignment

DIGITAL VIDEO 🖥

If you would be interested in watching Priscilla Shirer herself discuss the material in this *MasterWork* lesson—and more— go to *www.lifeway.com* and purchase your personal copy of the digital video for Session 6 of *He Speaks to Me.*

Godly *servanthood* means laying aside our desires in full pursuit of God's. We find true peace and contentment when we submit to God's assignment. To understand and accept the callings or assignments God has for us, we must first understand that we have been set up!

Turn to Ephesians 2:10 and fill in the blank below: "We are His creation—created in Christ Jesus for

good works, _____

so that we should walk in them."

"And Samuel said, 'Speak, for Your servant is listening'" (1 Sam. 3:10, NASB).

Samuel was a servant.

Friend, you were not placed in your family, in your neighborhood, or on your job by accident. Your existence is God-planned. Your past, present, and future are in His hands.

Gifted for His Purposes

As Christians, we have the privilege of fulfilling God's purposes (see Jer. 1:4-5). We can have confidence in submitting to God's assignments when we first understand that we each have gifts—specific abilities to grow and bless the kingdom of God.

Daily Bread

"God ... has ... called us with a holy calling, not according to our works, but according to His own purpose and grace, which was given to us in Christ Jesus before time began" (2 Tim. 1:8-9).

Read 1 Corinthians 12:4-11. Where do spiritual gifts

originate (v. 4)? _____

The word *gift* implies that we neither select nor deserve these by our own merit. Our gifts are an extension of God's grace. Actively using our gifts for God's glory fulfills our callings. Sometimes, however, we use our gifts for personal reward.

When I first began speaking, I learned that motivational speakers are in high demand. My bank account grew larger while my spirit grew less satisfied. I closed seminars feeling unfulfilled. Then one day the Lord spoke to my heart. He affirmed that He had given me the gift of public speaking but pointed out that I was using the talent for my own benefit rather than His kingdom. I struggled to give up my will and obey God's leading. But God continued to speak to me through Scripture, patiently bending me to His purposes by revealing His perspective.

My heart transition began when I read 2 Corinthians 5:1-9. Paul focused his attention on that which is eternal because he understood that "the earthly tent" or the things of this earth are only temporary.

According to 2 Corinthians 5:20, what is the role of an ambassador? _____

What a powerful reminder for me that my gifts have been given to fulfill His assignment. I simply needed to submit to it.

Read Romans 8:28. Our duty is to participate in what God has planned. What gifts has God given you that make your job(s) a good fit for you?

_____

How does living for God's purpose change the way you do your job?

_____

When you understand and accept your God-given assignment and begin to utilize your gifts to fulfill it, you will find contentment this world cannot provide.

Take Action

Close your study time in prayer. Honestly tell the Lord your response to His invitation to live for Him. Ask Him to use your gifts for His glory.

Then copy these statements onto a note card. Carry it with you and repeat them several times a day.

- *My life means more than the temporary.*

- *I live at this point in history for a reason.*

- *My existence is no mistake.*

- *I'm here for a purpose, to fulfill my God-given role!*

day Two

Submissive to the Lord's Challenges

Daily Bread

"In this world you will have trouble. But take courage. I have overcome the world" (John 16:33, NIV).

Today we focus on the fact that God's assignments do not come free from challenges. Hard times often come, either derailing us from the mission or making us more committed to following what God asks of us.

John 16:33 verifies that we will find suffering and trials in this life, but it also offers encouragement. Jesus has conquered the world. Through the power of His Holy Spirit, we too can triumph over difficulty.

What emotions do you normally experience when facing trouble? _____

What encouragement do you find in 1 Peter 4:12-13 concerning trouble?

_____

We can rest assured we find God orchestrating the events of our lives to build us up and bring Himself glory, but that doesn't mean we will always like what He has assigned us to do. The greatest challenge may be understanding that sometimes His assignments are different from our plans.

However, we can control our responses. We can rejoice in the good we know God will bring from hardship, and we can rejoice in the Lord Himself even when no good seems possible. Here are some reasons why.

A Matter of Perspective

As we submit to the Lord's plans, we must first allow God to change our perspective, radically realigning our desires with His. The challenges we face are spiritual exercises designed to make us stronger, making us more capable of fulfilling our God-given assignments.

Look at James 1:2-4 in the margin. Underline the attributes that God builds through trials.

The Greek word used for the word "trial" in James is *peirasmos.* This word means "experiment." The goal of an experiment is to validate a hypothesis or to experientially validate a set of theories that have not yet been proven true. Only through trials do we move from theoretical to practical faith. God sometimes wants to demonstrate to us truth about ourselves or Himself. Could viewing challenges as exercises given by your loving Father help to change your perspective on hardship?

You may still experience times of frustration, but a new perspective will change the way you handle negative feelings. Peter and the apostles continued in obedience to their God-given assignment in the face of many challenges and hardships. In fact, because they would not dismiss their calling and continued to preach the gospel of Jesus, they were brutally beaten.

Read Acts 5:41. What was their emotional response to this trial? _____

These men knew that obedience to God was more important than pleasing men or protecting their own comfort and safety (see Acts 5:29).

Write in the margin a challenge you are facing. Write at least one life lesson this challenge is teaching you.

Knowing challenges are developing character enables us to change our emotional response to trials.

A Matter of Focus

We need to keep our eyes focused on eternity. In light of the great reward that awaits those who suffer for the sake of Christ, our challenges shrink. Second Corinthians 4:17 says that "our momentary light affliction is producing for us an absolutely incomparable eternal weight of glory."

I once heard speaker Cal Thomas illustrate this well. He explained that if he were staying in a hotel room where he didn't like the decor or carpet, it would be silly for him to get frustrated and upset and call the manager

"Consider it a great joy, my brothers, whenever you experience various trials, knowing that the testing of your faith produces endurance. But endurance must do its complete work, so that you may be mature and complete, lacking nothing" (Jas. 1:2-4).

to complain about his surroundings. It would be a much better use of his time and energy to simply endure the ugly decor and remember that he is only passing through. Keep your eyes focused on your real home—heaven. Don't get so frustrated with life that you forget you are passing through.

Rewrite Philippians 3:20 in one sentence or less using your own words.

In the margin, write a Scripture to share with your group that helps you keep an eternal perspective.

A Matter of Security

The silversmith watches the metal, prepared to take it out at just the right moment. Too much heat will damage the precious work. God is the divine silversmith (see Mal. 3:3). When we are burdened, broken, and in need, God reminds us we are not alone. He watches over us and He knows when enough is enough.

Do you know how the silversmith knows the refining process is complete? He must be able to clearly see his reflection in the molten metal. We sometimes find ourselves in a place we believe is too difficult. The intense heat seems to be too much to bear, but God is paying close attention. His work will be done when He can see His reflection in us.

In what ways have your challenges made you more

Christlike?_____

Take Action

Read Thessalonians 5:18. Close your time of Bible study today with your own thanksgiving service. Think carefully about the current challenges you face and give thanks to God especially for those things. Thank Him for how He is using those as experiments to build you up and that you can count on His presence to be with you through the whole thing! Thank Him for heaven and the promise of eternity with Him.

day Three

Submissive to the Lord's Desires

In Psalm 37:4, printed in the margin, underline what we must do to receive our hearts' desires.

Daily Bread

"Delight yourself in the LORD; and He will give you the desires of your heart" (Ps. 37:4, NASB).

The Hebrew word used for "delight" in Psalm 37:4 is *anag*. It means "to make merry over, to take exquisite delight." Delighting in God is a natural reaction from enthusiastic, spiritually hungry, and passionate people so in love with God that they want to please Him in every way. Delighting ourselves in the Lord results in action.

Read Acts 16:22-32. In the midst of a difficult situation Paul and Silas delighted themselves in God. What happened as a result of their focus?

_____

Delight and Righteousness

Psalm 37:4 says that when we delight in the Lord He will grant us the desires of our hearts. When we delight in Him, we develop the kind of righteous desires God wants to grant.

Note that desire follows delighting in God. If God granted our desires without our delighting in Him first, our desires would often lead us in the wrong direction. We would miss God's best.

See Psalm 84:11 in the margin. Underline the promise.

God responds to integrity. Apart from an intimate relationship with God, the heart desires things contrary to God's desire. My angry heart seeks revenge. My lustful heart brings to my mind compromising situations.

Recall a time when your relationship with God was lacking. How did your desires evidence this fact?

_____

Our desires most closely align with God's when we delight in Him. This truth makes itself evident in my own life. It surprises me how drastically my desires conform to a completely different standard when I am wrapped up in God. When I delight in Him, the rebel in me desires to submit, the stressed mother in me desires to be more patient, and the jealous sister in me desires to befriend the target of her jealousy.

"For the LORD God is a sun and shield. The LORD gives grace and glory; He does not withhold the good from those who live with integrity" (Ps. 84:11).

Take Action

Be honest with the Lord. Tell Him how you feel about Him. Ask Him to give you the inner fervor to delight in Him. Express to Him your desperation to know and understand His desires for you. Submit your desires and look forward to them changing to match His. For additional Scripture examples of obedience preceding blessing, study the following passages: Psalm 37:4-5,27,34; Isaiah 58:14; James 4:7; 1 Peter 5:6.

163

Submissive to the Lord's Authority

Daily Bread
"I want you to know that Christ is the head of every man, and the man is the head of the woman, and God is the head of Christ" (I Cor. 11:3).

The word *submission* conjures images of door mats and prison bars. Most of us don't like submission, and we don't want to submit. Perhaps we don't even know how. But if we want to hear God's voice and experience His best, we must learn to willingly submit to His authority. As a woman I want to stress that God calls everyone to submit.

Read the following verses and check to whom the author is speaking.

	Males	Females	Married	Both
1 Peter 5:5				
James 4:7				
Hebrews 13:17				
1 Peter 2:18				
Ephesians 5:22				
Romans 13:1				

The process of submitting implies a willingness on our part to yield. You may have been surprised to discover that only one of the passages on submission deals with married women.

In the margin list the authorities God has placed over you. What might your submission to their authority show God about how you will respond to Him?

Our Problem with Submission

Why is the foundational principle of submission so difficult? The answer is found in two words—human nature! We want to have our own way, and we become angry and resentful when we don't get it. Submission to